JOB INTERVIEW

Step Guide on How to Prepare for Job Interview

(Stand Out From the Crowd and Crack Your First Job Interview)

Robbin Desilets

Published by Bengion Cosalas

Robbin Desilets

All Rights Reserved

Job Interview: Step Guide on How to Prepare for Job Interview (Stand Out From the Crowd and Crack Your First Job Interview)

ISBN 978-1-77485-316-0

All rights reserved. No part of this guide may be reproduced in any form without permission in writing from the publisher except in the case of brief quotations embodied in critical articles or reviews.

Legal & Disclaimer

The information contained in this book is not designed to replace or take the place of any form of medicine or professional medical advice. The information in this book has been provided for educational and entertainment purposes only.

The information contained in this book has been compiled from sources deemed reliable, and it is accurate to the best of the Author's knowledge; however, the Author cannot guarantee its accuracy and validity and cannot be held liable for any errors or omissions. Changes are periodically made to this book. You must consult your doctor or get professional medical advice before using any of the suggested remedies, techniques, or information in this book.

Upon using the information contained in this book, you agree to hold harmless the Author from and against any damages, costs, and expenses, including any legal fees potentially resulting from the application of any of the information provided by this guide. This disclaimer applies to any damages or injury caused by the use and application, whether directly or indirectly, of any advice or information presented, whether for breach of contract, tort, negligence, personal injury, criminal intent, or under any other cause of action.

You agree to accept all risks of using the information presented inside this book. You need to consult a professional medical practitioner in order to ensure you are both able and healthy enough to participate in this program.

Table of Contents

INTRODUCTION 1

CHAPTER 1: PRIOR RESEARCH 10

CHAPTER 2: PREPARING FOR THE JOB INTERVIEW 21

CHAPTER 3: PRACTICAL HINTS FOR PREPARATION 27

CHAPTER 4: WHAT'S YOUR MOST FLAW? 49

CHAPTER 5: THE REASONS COMPANIES CONDUCT GROUP INTERVIEWS 56

CHAPTER 6: QUESTIONS TO TEST COMMITMENT AND MOTIVATION 67

CHAPTER 7: SPREADING THE WORD - FEEL THE POWER OF AFFIRMATIONS AND SUBLIMINALS 77

CHAPTER 8: BEFORE THE INTERVIEW 86

CHAPTER 9: THE COVER LETTER 101

CHAPTER 10: THE INTERVIEW PROCESS 107

CHAPTER 11: WHAT TO DISCUSS 127

CHAPTER 12: WHAT IS THE REASON FINDING A JOB IS IMPORTANT? 131

CHAPTER 13: BEING CONFIDENT 137

CHAPTER 14: SAMPLE THANK-YOU LETTERS................... 145

CHAPTER 15: PRACTICE IS THE KEY TO PERFECTING YOUR SKILLS.. 161

CHAPTER 16: COMMON INTERVIEW MISTAKES............. 177

CONCLUSION.. 183

Introduction

The abilities required to make an impression on others and how we present ourselves in the interview are similar to the abilities that allow us to feel confident making friends in any social setting. If you are able to create a positive impression on others, and how to make an impact on others and make yourself appear as an engaging and skilled individual, you'll be extremely well, not only in the interview, but also in everyday life. Some of the more confident and enthusiastic of applicants might be nervous prior to entering the interviewing room. There's nothing wrong with that. It's just a natural thing to feel. It's important to know how to effectively and confidently present yourself with lots of enthusiasm. In reality, interviews for jobs are often viewed as an inconvenience and are the main obstacle that stands in the way of getting that job that we really would like.

A person's ability to do well in the interview is a important aspect of their future development of their career. The candidate must present the contribution they make to the team's efforts and also their individual capabilities, skills and capabilities. This means that you must prepare to the interview and prepare as best way you can.

Be aware that you'll do majority of the talking during an interview. That means that you could influence how the interview will go. While it is true that not every interview will go well, however it can be an extremely valuable experience to use for your next one. This is why you must present yourself in the most professional way possible and think of each interview as an excellent experience to gain knowledge.

The right mindset to achieve success is essential. We all know that you may have a high potential and have the skills to make your career progress but without the right mental attitude, reaching the target could not be as straightforward as you'd hoped. Being able to present yourself professionally in an interview requires many capabilities, confidence, and, of course, mental strength. It is essential to understand what prospective employers are actually seeking. You have the capacity to change your mind's focus to be positive rather than negative. It is a fact we are more in control on our thoughts and emotions than others believe.

What's the goal of an interview? You'd like the interviewer to feel that you understand your work well, and that you're committed, reliable, and honest and trustworthy too. It is important to keep in mind that if you fail to excel at work, your career as a manager will suffer, which means that the person will be more cautious in the hiring process. What they're seeking is a candidate who is educated as well as professional experience that is relevant and someone they would be able to admire.

Everyone is stressed, it's an everyday thing. Some of us experience it more frequently, to others it's more common while to others more. But the best part is that we have control over it. Each of us has one chance. Each of us has numerous chances to be successful. Remember this and you'll discover your life is less stressful. This is also true for those dreadful job interviews. Before you go to the interview, take the burden off of your shoulders by saying to you: "I will have other interviews following this one. Therefore, there's no reason to get anxious. This isn't my chance to be a failure!"

I cannot stress enough how important it is to be able to develop a mentality. What exactly is a growth mindset?

I'm glad that you asked! It's a fervent belief that you're in charge of your life, and that you have the ability to continuously develop and grow. This is the foundation to achievement. Naturally, dedication, hard work and drive to be successful as well as perseverance are essential however, understanding that you're in charge of your destiny is essential.

Knowing that your entire life doesn't depend entirely on what happens in your interview will help you feel more comfortable and will improve the chances of showing yourself as you would like to. In this moment it could be an excellent idea to look around and reflect about the way you live your life. You've lived for all these years without a job, don't you think? What if the world truly come an end if you do not grasp it? We all know that answer but you have to say it loudly. It's a big fat NO! I'm not saying that this job isn't crucial to you, obviously but it is important to move away from your goals while helping you tremendously in managing the stress that you're experiencing.

It's perfectly normal that we make mistakes from time time, but it's important to learn from the mistakes. We've all made a number of mistakes in a variety of situations however, the effort to gain something from each failure is priceless. Every failure is an opportunity to learn. So, we all learn from every situation where we didn't get a chance to present ourselves good as we had hoped we could. You've attended job interviews before. If you feel you didn't make the cut do not feel guilty. Let's look at it this way: do not feel guilty. I have found that every loss can be one you can take advantage of if you're willing for learning from the mistakes you made. Everyone has had a setback at in some way or another Don't be a victim to yourself. Don't be discouraged, look at what went wrong, and decide what you could do different in the coming years and then just get on with it. There's a saying that says that the things that will determine your potential to be successful aren't your wins but how you deal with your loss. Being flexible is vitally important. Being able to remain focussed on the goals and be able to roll with the punches is crucial to remain on the road to success.

The way we think is crucial. In many cases, we are the ones we are most at risk of and think negatively about our capabilities and our future. It is essential to be aware of the words we speak to ourselves. Positive thinking is essential for us to succeed in the world that can be very difficult and harsh. Thus, the results we get in this world are dependent on our manner of thinking! Encourage yourself. Do not be afraid to praise yourself, especially when you feel that you deserve it. Give yourself a treat from time the time. However, this doesn't mean that you have to be apathetic and unfocused. Staying focused on your goals is essential.

If you are feeling anxious about your job interview, keep in mind that the anxiety is stemming from your thoughts, not from the circumstances. It is certainly important for you to land your job but just take the time to think what's the worst thing that could occur? If this interview does not happen as I expected and they do not like me, then what? There are many other opportunities and it's not an end in itself. However it doesn't matter if you've have had a bad incident in the past does not mean that it will be the same in the future. If the interview did not go according to plan , or you felt that you should have been more prepared, try to be compassionate to yourself. Don't be too hard on yourself Everyone makes mistakes at times. Spend the time you're able to on reviewing how you can improve in the future.

Tips for interviewing:

Don't dwell on the past. Even if you didn't seem as successful at previous interviews, it does not mean that the next one will be any different. You learn and get better.

Most people who were ever employed had to pass an interview process to be considered for the job. So don't be afraid; it's simply an interview. Don't be afraid to decline an interview because of your age.

Feel scared. This job may prove to be the perfect fit for you. The most important message you wish to send is that you're an ideal candidate to do the job. To achieve that you must convince the employer that have plenty to offer. Be sure to spend the time to think about your along with your talents and the strengths you have. This will assist you in discover the most effective method to demonstrate why you're the right person for the position.

Chapter 1: Prior Research

If you want to be successful in an interview, the very first step you must take is to ensure that you are taking advantage of the benefit of knowing all you can about the person you are interviewing. Along with giving you to a degree in confidence, it provides you a sense of how to respond to questions, and more generally, how you effectively present yourself during the interview. If the interviewer or employer observes that you are familiar with the organization and the company, you instantly become an exceptional candidate.

A summary of prior research prior to stepping into an interview can aid you:

Answer more in depth questions on why you're a great match for the company.

Show enthusiasm and a high level of interest and enthusiasm for the position

Show professionalism and advocacy

In the process of preparing to interview for the job, I've compiled the following points that are important to learn about the potential employer:

Its mission, abilities and values of the business

The mission statement of the business is, in the first place crucial because it gives you a glimpse of the company's values (more about this later) and the core values they require you to exhibit (it will help in preparing for interview questions).

The website of the company is an excellent resource to read about their mission statement. If you read their mission statement, make sure to connect your job with it. Also, be aware of your experiences and education to assist the organization meet its objectives.

When you are preparing for a conversation about the mission statement, think about the mission statement in the form of discussion structure to ensure that, when you are asked this question in your interview you are not able to simply say it.

You can go further and identify the expertise and experience that the company's values. It is here that you can look at the nuances of their job announcements. Get more details from the careers page of the employer to be able to know what kind of employee they're looking for. In the end, you can reach out to some of your employees currently employed and ask them what their company's values are in its workplace.

I have to affirm that the mission and values aren't difficult to find since they are often prominently displayed on company websites under the "About Us" section. The majority of the time all you have to do is to study the content carefully to find out how distinct the business is from other companies. For instance, if are interviewing a marketing agency, you'll notice that "committed to providing excellent customer service" is a characteristic that its rivals boast However, if the company has "sustainability" as a secondary quality, it is important to take note of.

Make sure you review all of this, along with other fundamentals you must know before the interview, including the history and the size of the company and its location. You don't want to be the one who is unable to answer an inquiry (or is asked a question) which is answered found on the homepage of the website.

Culture of the company

It can be difficult to comprehend the culture of a business without talking with employees or visiting the offices of the company. However it is possible to get some idea about how the organisation wants people to see their work and their culture. To find out the only thing you require to do is use social media.

Many companies are currently posting the same information on Twitter, Facebook,

LinkedIn, Instagram, and so on, showcasing their social gatherings, employees and more and are all essential elements of their company culture. Find it. Are they calm, casualor?

Once you have this information then, all you have to do is apply this information to show yourself as someone who is a good fit in the culture of the company. For instance, "I would want to join the team since the culture is really lively, enjoyable and modern!"

Products, clients, services, as well as competitors

I'm sure I don't need to talk about this, however, to emphasize its significance however, I'll mention it. It is essential to be aware of the kind of work you'll be performing in the event of being hired, what products and services that the business provides, as well as its clients. Knowing this information alone will aid you in answering hundreds of questions during an interview.

For more details about the offerings of the company visit their website and go through cases studies, blogs and white papers. It is important to convince the interviewer that you are aware of the particular niche that the business seeks to fill. This requires knowing your competitors. Knowing the competition will put you in a higher position since it shows that you are knowledgeable about the entire industry.

Be sure to search for the major firms that are linked to the business. Sometimes, this could be as easy as searching for companies in the same area however most of the time it will require a bit more searching. Does the company have any lost contracts? If yes Who was the winner? If you've got a solid understanding of the competitors, you can utilize this information to answer questions regarding the company's position and your primary motivation or reason for joining the business, the uniqueness of the business and its products, and most importantly, what you will do to aid the growth of the business within the market.

The financial health of the company

If you're on the website of your company go to the tab labelled "investor relations" (or any similar). A majority of companies hold quarterly earnings conferences and annual reports that are available to customers (and potential investors).

The reports and calls generally include a variety of topics that are otherwise difficult to find. This includes it includes company risks or new products as well as the rates of growth in revenue. Another good spot to verify if you're conducting interviews with startups company is Crunchbase. There, you can find many details about current stages of capital raising, new hires as well as acquisitions, and useful news coverage.

If you have the data then it's your responsibility to make your own decisions. It is not necessary to give a detailed account of the history of funding or the stock price but you'll be more successful if you can provide a clear and concise explanation of what you believe the company's position will be within a specific time frame, backed by evidence. This will certainly be a big hit with any professional interviewer.

The interviewer

As you know that interviewers are hiring individuals and not resumes. This means that if they are able to interview three applicants who are qualified they have to pick the candidate with whom they have the strongest relationship. Thus, getting acquainted with the person you are interviewing with prior to the interview is crucial.

Before your interview day you should look up details about the person you will be interviewing. Begin with the job advertisement or email, then begin digging. There is a wealth of relevant information through Facebook and

LinkedIn regarding your person(s) who is conducting the interview.

So, what should you search for?

You must know your background, interests, and objectives so that you are aware of the best way to lead the conversation, what to mention, and what examples to utilize. For instance, if the person you interview has a goat for his profile picture on Facebook and you own a Billy similar to the breed, you can make use of this little tidbit of information in order to establish relationships.

Remember to do it intuitively and naturally. I can't imagine how awkward it could be if you started making unintentional remarks about how much are a goat lover!

What's going on in the company currently? It's a constant challenge for recruiters to bring new employees up to speed on the latest happenings within the company. A smart candidate will beat this obstacle by staying up-to-date with the latest developments. No matter if the business has recently has completed a merger, or is planning to launch a brand new service knowing about it will give you an edge. This information will allow you to ease the stress of telling about everything. It will show yourself as a competent and diligent employee while also impressing the interviewer with your expertise.

With the advent of the internet, it's easy to track down any company's current or future activities. Simply search Google for any relevant news articles or press announcements. The company's website and social media channels are likely to offer you additional information on this subject.

Although there are numerous other aspects you can look up prior to entering the interview but these are the most crucial ones to begin with. When you've prepared with this method you will not have a problem getting it wrong!

Don't forget the goal you're trying to achieve is to sound as convincing as you can when you declare, "I want to be part of the team." Make sure you support this by describing the uniqueness of the company and show your excitement to be a part of it by telling them that you are as knowledgeable about the company as anyone else currently working for the organization.

Include pertinent examples that show what you are aware about the company in order to answer any interview questions.

Let's take a look at the best ways to respond to a range of questions that interviewers might ask:

Chapter 2: Preparing For The Job Interview

What do you need to bring?

Making yourself aware of what you will talk about before, during, and following the interview isn't the only factor to think about as there are many items to be prepared prior to going to an interview. In this section we'll go over what you need to know about the items you should be prepared for your job interview.

Two copies of the resume

You are aware of the importance of an effective resume and how vital it is to set it together in the correct way, but you must be aware that you should always carry several copies in case you are going to an interview. What's the point? Why is it important to have multiple resumes? It's a question you won't be able to tell! What happens if there's an interview panel present? Then, submitting your resume to each interviewer will provide them with the impression that you're always ready.

It's also a good idea it is possible that you will find another job opening for a different company which you could submit your resume.

A pen and notebook

This allows you to keep track of the important things the interviewer mentions in the course of an interview. It is also possible to write down any questions you'd like to ask your interviewer when you are ready to speak. After the interview is over you could sit in a quiet spot and record your impressions about the organization, the concerns they raised, and the positive aspects of the interview and those you could improve upon. It is possible to be disciplined when noting down notes, but can you imagine how prepared you'll feel when they call you to schedule another interview? You'll feel sure that you'll be a success at any interview.

Snacks and books

Why are these things could you wonder. It is possible that you will have to wait until your turn to be interviewed, so to prevent boredom bring something to keep you entertained in the form of reading documents. Also, you don't want to attend an interview if you're hungry.

The Right Bag

It's essential that you carry the correct bag to an interview. For males, it's recommended to carry an authentic leather briefcase, and for women, a bag that can be carried on the shoulder could be a nice option. Be sure the bag you choose to use is stylish and can carry everything you require.

If you can prepare these tasks that appear to be insignificant tasks, you improve your chances of being selected for the job you're seeking.

Proper Clothing

If you're attending an interview for a job You're likely conscious of the necessity to dress appropriately to create a positive impression on the person you are interviewing with. It's common sense since the primary goal for you to do is impress your prospective employer, and convey the impression that you are the ideal person for this job. Here are some guidelines you can be aware of when selecting the appropriate clothes to your visit.

For Men:

Long sleeves with the right neck tie

If you're used to wearing a basic shirt or polo shirt, you should change your clothes if you're attending a job interview. You must dress professionally and professional, so wearing long sleeves and a tie can make you appear professional.

Slacks

Jeans are a huge no-no during job interviews. Instead, opt to wear slacks and wear long-sleeved.

Black leather shoes

The look of leather shoes at your interview is sure to enhance your look. Be sure to wear black socks to appear neat and tidy.

For women:

Formal top

Long sleeves in white and an edgy black blazer for cover-ups will always be effective. This outfit will help you appear serious about the job that you're applying for.

Slacks or pencil skirt

The skirt you wear should be at least at knee level because you don't want your skirt to look too sexually attractive to your prospective employer. If you're looking to be safe, you should put on slacks instead.

High heels, but not too high

It's fine to wear shoes two or three inches of heels, but anything more than that can make you appear to be going to a party , rather than an interview.

Light makeup

The application of makeup will offer you a more lively appearance however, be careful not to apply excessively vibrant red lipstick or eye shadow. A light makeup can enhance your overall appearance.

These are the most important points to be aware of when going to an interview for a job. Always keep in mind that you're making an impression on your potential employer and your coworkers so make sure you look your best. It's not necessary to spend an enormous amount of money on an expensive dress so long as you appear professional, neat and attractive and professional, you're in good shape.

Chapter 3: Practical Hints for Preparation

We've now discussed the mindset for interviewing (which as with all habits is not formed over night) We can move on to the less important tips. These tips can be helpful but only when they're implemented with an appropriate mindset. We will nevertheless investigate these tips.

It is often the case that when we notice advertisements from a company in the paper We think it's an excellent opportunity to be able to apply and get into the company.

However, it is important to remember it was actually the business who published the need for employees instead of the reverse. If they weren't urgently in need of skilled workers then they wouldn't published the news.

The first obstacle has been addressed. It is important to remember that they depend on you, and not vice versa. Sure, you require work that pays but it's their need that is more important than your own. When you first look up the job posting for interviews and you are able to prepare yourself to seize the opportunity with both hands.

As opposed to focusing on the way you can make money from having the job and not focusing on the fact that jobs are about providing a reward for an organization as well as their customers.

Being prepared for an interview by having your perspective on how you'll offer an incentive to the organization will allow you to view the task from a completely different angle.

Many people who have constant health problems, generally have a low confidence in themselves due to physical constraints. When stress related to money and debts that are not paid are added to the mix and the result is greater mental strain. If you are more desperate than feel for job, the more anxious you could appear and even become in the process of interviewing. You might feel that you must request or even ask for something you want instead of providing your abilities.

Have a look at your work as a fair trade. With this arrangement, you will trade your expertise and potential for a salary in exchange for fair pay and the chance to discover something new. It's more rational than just looking at the scenario as if you were searching for a job and desperately trying to get through the process of interviewing to secure it. You'll be amazed by this newfound certainty you've achieved, only by reaching this simple conclusion, will boost confidence in yourself.

The people who work for organizations are individuals. The characters of these individuals are often a part of their culture of work. If you do a little research ahead of time you can identify the most important aspects of their corporate personality. This puts you ahead of others who are looking for an opportunity.

Important Answers

The most frequent question asked during an interview , is "Why do you require to work here?" Now, you could go in either direction when answering this question, honest or not. A lot of people talk about why they require money to pay their past due bills, or need to improve their health benefits or even talk about how close their workplace is close to their homes.

If you're looking to make a statement about how bills that haven't been paid have been a constant source of stress for months and the severity of a financial crisis you're in it is the game in a fair way and the right way. While there is truth in this statement but it's not going to suffice. Employers aren't concerned with the story about why you're looking for work. They're more interested in what you can offer your prospective employer or what's the best thing you can do for them.

Another question that is both annoying and important frequently requested by prospective employers would be "What is your greatest strength?" Now, the most obvious method to answer this question is to list all the positive areas of not only the academics you have, but your personality. However, every other applicant will be doing the exact process. Instead, you should focus on your own personal qualities over the ones already included on your resume. If you choose to do this you're showing your employer a side of you that isn't previously displayed. If you show your employer that you're more than your marks and grades and points, it creates a trust in them.

In the same way, a lot of interviewers inquire about your weak points. They don't want to discover where you're lacking. The purpose behind asking the question is to find out whether you're aware of your shortcomings or not. When inquired on your strengths, and answer by saying "none," there is an excellent chance of getting disqualified immediately. Be honest when you answer the question, because once you've been hired, your employer is likely to discover your weaknesses in the end. It is therefore more effective if they're ready to handle them instead of astonishing them and enduring the negative reaction. So, it's better to be honest rather than sorry. It also lets them know that you're cognizant of weaknesses and your strengths. This is crucial when it comes to work.

A well-written CV

A CV is your resume when you're in search of the job. It reflects your skills in a way that you would not be competent to convey during a personal interview. It's the primary document that proves your credentials and showcases your abilities to those in a position to offer you an opportunity. It is crucial to begin working towards making a solid CV during your school days. Participating in good institutions and presenting studies on your subject, as well as working under knowledgeable and famous people from your field are a few of the most important aspects that a competitive CV must include.

A CV is a formal evidence that proves you have the required skills and abilities to fulfill the task. There are a few basic points that you should take into consideration when preparing of the CV.

The program you're pursuing must be in line with the position you're looking for. Select a program that is composed of as many different degrees as is possible. In some cases, the presence of a combined degree earns you points even though the individual degrees that are integrated may not be a good possibility of securing work, if examined as a whole.

A great CV includes references from all the appropriate locations. It is highly recommended to do an internship and gain experience with people and organizations that are important and are able to stand the scrutiny of those who might be interviewing you. If the people who are established in the industry say that you're competent in your job, that is a huge factor when you embark looking for jobs. With their support you have a better chance of getting the job that you desire.

It's also crucial to have a neat and clear format. Anyone who said that looks aren't important have never had a badly structured resume. Resumes are supposed to impress the reader and a poorly formatted resume and a font that isn't right can hinder your chances of being able to attend an interview or even get the job. Let your resume stand out.

Be honest

One of the most important things to keep in mind when updating the resume of yours is to remember that lying could end up slicing into your back in the end. Many companies have a practice of conducting background checks on those who apply for jobs with them. If they find anything that is false or perhaps not reliable and they are able to not just deny your application. The majority of companies have databases of fraudulent applicants which is distributed through the entire process of businesses. People who are known to be lying are banned immediately and every company is likely to look up your name into the database to see if you've been lying on your resumes. If your name is entered in the database mentioned and is there for a long time, it's for the rest of time. Therefore, being untrue in your resume won't just end your current job as well as limit any future opportunities that you be offered.

It is essential to proofread.

If you are submitting your resume to a prospective employer to review ensure that at least two persons go through the resume in the hopes of identifying any factual or grammatical mistakes. A single typo could make it impossible for you to get an interview because it demonstrates a lack of professionalism on your part.

Do your homework

It's not enough to have a great CV is prepared. It must be followed with a substantial amount of research and background checks of the organization you're applying for an employment. Being aware of their background, the establishment on facts, merger policies , and other important information regarding the company will be useful when you're asked to an interview. Being familiar with the company's history and the nature of work puts you in a favorable way and communicates towards the person interviewing you that shows that you're really keen to work with them. This increases your chances of being selected if you demonstrate how you are knowledgeable about the company and their work.

The D-Day

An interview should examine your abilities on the actual aspects of the game, and check the assertions you have made on your resume. It is crucial that the interview is successful.

First of all, dress appropriate in the event of an interview. For the most part, casual wear works all the time. If a particular colour or code of dress is required, stick to it according to its requirements. Don't mismatch your socks and tie and definitely do not go for bright and gaudy colors that could blind butterflies. It is recommended to choose neutral colored suits that give an appearance of professionalism. Make sure to take care of your personal hygiene prior to going into the interview area. A soiled or unkempt beard, a dirty manicure and dirty noses can be a turnoff for employers. They're not just a negative reflection on your appearance, but also reflect your character in the eyes of society. A person who is well-groomed and dressed like gentlemanly is more likely to be preferred over someone who didn't have the time to do some self-improvement.

Check that your posture moving around, sitting down and standing up is perfectly suited to your body, then at the very least not worthy of criticism from judges. Your posture reflects your attitude towards things generally. A relaxed sitting posture conveys a sense of disdain, whereas an attitude of complete attention conveys positive energy.

Another crucial aspect of interviewing is how you communicate. How you communicate reveals to a great deal about who you are. Use a lively, formal tone such as - "I'd like to look into this possibility" and not "Yeah it would be great to work alongside you."

When you are speaking to the people who are conducting your interview, you should look at them with a straight face and be confident in your speech. Your voice should show the fact that you're aware of your capabilities and are confident in your abilities. Avoid excessive pomp and exaggeration when asked to talk about your self. Interviews typically begin with a warm up questions like "tell us something about your personal characteristics."

Be sure to be concise and prompt when responding to this kind of questions. These questions are meant to help you feel relaxed prior to the interview progressing to further discussions and technical questions. Limit the duration of your response to these inquiries up to 30 seconds. A brief, but complete explanation of your interests and achievements should be provided. Nobody will have any further questions about this information since it's an exercise to warm up.

Admit your faults

If, during your interview, you're shocked by a question you don't know the answer to It is detrimental to your chances of continuing to and keep beating around the subject rather than admitting that you aren't sure. The flimsiest of attempts to dodge questions never impress interviewers. If you can be honest and say apology, "I'm sorry, sir I'm sorry, but I've got no idea. This could help you gain points. Also, it can add the bonus points If you are politely asking the conductor for the correct answer after admitting your ignorance.

Businesses reward those who love to learn , and disapprove of people who simply try to make a mess out of a circumstance or simply talk about things they don't know what the answer is to. Your curiosity gives you an advantage over those who did not bother to ask questions and then sulked that they were not good at it.

Skill-sets

Employers always look for candidates with a base set of abilities. These include the ability to think logically, communicate technological accuracy, and interpersonal capabilities.

Logical thinking refers to the capacity of our minds to make decisions and make choices using the power of reasoning. Inductive reasoning, deductive and adductive capabilities form a fundamental logic set. It is not everyone who is capable to think logically in challenging circumstances and unexpected situations. The more reasoning exhibited by a prospective employee, the better the chance of being hired.

Communication skills are essential to be successful in the job interview. If you're not able to communicate your issues to your employer and other employees in a timely manner that you can, then you're likely not the best candidate to do the job. A relationship between an employee and employer requires the disclosure of specific actions in a timely manner to an employer. Doing something that is not in the company's favor or not letting him know about the important facts that could be detrimental to the company's reputation is thought as a sign of a lack of the ability to communicate.

The ability to communicate with technical accuracy is a fundamental necessity. You might be a fantastic person, and possess an I.Q. of more than 130, however, when you don't get the nuts and bolts that are technical right, you'll be pruned right from the start. Being technically proficient requires that your foundations solid.

The job of the bank could require you to be adept at math and accounting. For instance, a law firm could require you to be familiar with constitution or state laws.

An occupation is not just simply doing work and receiving a salary. It is a place of work with numerous other employees working alongside you. It is a rule of thumb to be a worker not only for your employers, but for your fellow colleagues. Interviewers will want to gauge your social skills by asking you about your friends circle, or what you do during your time off. The use of hypothetical questions that are based on imagined scenarios are also expected.

Internships

Internships can be a fantastic method to make contact with a company before you begin thinking about being employed by them. A job internship doesn't just give you recommendations, but it can also help you adjust to the workplace and the culture. It allows you to get acquainted with your fellow workers and the nature of their jobs.

This will help you decide whether you'd like to be employed in the area or not. Internships in a company is possible during the college holidays or in part-time if your college and work environment permit it. Begin by volunteering to help with the work and, eventually, when they begin to notice your work and want to pay you. Volunteering shows your dedication to the task. Companies will look into their internship boxes for possible future opportunities. It's a cost-effective means of ensuring that they continue offering employment. Interns are more desirable than other applicants at any time.

Personal touch

If you are able contact the HR department of the business you're interested in working for. While it might sound like a negative approach but you could try using your personal connections with them to secure an employment opportunity with the business. You shouldn't feel ashamed about accepting a job that was arranged through personal connections. In the end, it's Darwinism at its very best. The fact that you're well-known to those who hire you can give you an edge during the interview However, don't take it as a given.

Right Approach

Make an impression on the interviewer by using your wit and the cool way of approaching. Many interviewers attempt to catch candidates off guard by asking questions that are unconventional and scenarios. An example scenario is presented and the applicant is then asked to think about what he would react in the scenario. A calm and funny approach to answering these questions will improve your chances. Don't be anxious and let the unpredictability of the question overwhelm you. Use a bit of common sense , and you'll be flying through these questions.

Begin by taking the first step.

If you're working on a trial-based basis or when you are an intern, you should request work. It is not in your best interests to sit at your desk all day perusing the Internet since no job was attributable to you. Make a statement and request work. If you need to, pressure your boss to give you a job and let him know that you don't wish to be idle and ineffective. Always appear working on something.

Choose a position that is interesting to you

Don't look for lucrative jobs that pay high salaries when you're not certain you're willing to dedicate your time to the task on the first place. Being able to perform work is not the same thing as being able to think about it. If you're not the type of person who is drawn to the same thing every day and you don't want to submit an application for one. Instead, find jobs that challenge you to think outside of the cubicle.

Negotiations

The most important part of your interview usually happens after the interview. This is when you're asked about the compensation portion of your job. Interviewers may provide ball park numbers. If the interviewer simply giving you the number you are entitled to then you are left with no option but to either accept the offer or not. This is especially true for jobs that advertise explicitly specified the exact amount you'll be receiving. There's a hint of "no negotiations" in this advertisement and you'd have seen it. It is therefore unprofessional to even try negotiating in such a situation.

But, if the job's announcement or notice did not mention pay, it's assumed that they will be open to engaging you in negotiations over the matter. Here are some guidelines you should remember when you negotiate:

Remember your strengths as well as your accomplishments and experiences prior to making a list of numbers. Your resume must be able to justify the amount you're quoting. If you make a statement that is over what you appear to be entitled to, it could cause the interviewer to be offended. If you also quote the wrong amount of money and it is not just going to cause you to be disadvantaged and your employer, but also be perceived as foolish by others around you.

Do not quote the amount of your compensation by yourself. Always remain polite and inquire with the interviewer what they believe you are due according to your resume and how you performed in the interview.

If you've received an amount you're not satisfied with, say your feelings in a way that doesn't show displeasure or displeasure.

Inform the interviewers of your previous jobs and the amount you were paid. Sometimes, you can be a little generous with this number since cross-checking the salary of applicants in their previous jobs isn't an usual method. However, it is important to play carefully in case you are caught this could cause you to be blocked.

Always inquire if the amount you're offered comes with tax cuts or not. The typical salary in your employment contract is higher than what you actually receive. This is due to various taxation, 401(k) or similar reductions. Be sure to know the benefits you will receive before you sign up.

Chapter 4: What's Your Most Flaw?

Like the earlier question on strengths, when the interviewer asks you identify your biggest weakness it is self-reflection. Are you able to recognize your weaknesses and confident enough to express your weaknesses?

This is a question that's designed to prompt you to think about it and delve on your soul and conduct some serious soul-searching. If you're trying to perform all the soul-searching and thinking tasks in your interview with no prior planning, then the process could be quite frightening and could lead to some anxious moments.

Common Faults

"My weaknesses are actually my strength!"

You've probably read many books, blogs, or articles in which they advise you to choose an area of strength, and present it as your biggest weaknesses. For example,

"My greatest weakness is that I'm an perfectionist." It's a pity! This is not the best approach to answer this question. The first thing to note is that picking your strengths and presenting that it is a weakness is a false assumption. It also ignores the purpose in the interview. Thirdly, you could physically harm the interviewer when the eyes of the interviewer roll back the head!

The question may sound odd, but it serves a important purpose. The interviewer doesn't care the answer you give; (s)he actually wants to examine how you respond! It's an excellent chance for you to transform the seemingly irrelevant question into an important break to clearly portray you as the most qualified candidate for the job.

Have no fear!

Don't be afraid to acknowledge that you're not the perfect person. Since, in the end, every imperfection comes the possibility of development. The trick is to identify the weaknesses. If you can identify your weaknesses or personality flaws, for instance you will be able to work on them or at a minimum, work around them. Let's say for instance, that you don't really do well as a team member or that you're not your most efficient delegator. What better way to admit this? Recognize that you're having trouble trusting the most critical tasks to other people until you're sure of their skills and their standards.

Answering the Question : What is your biggest weakness?

We all like to admit we are not perfect. of shortcomings. However, you have to face your weaknesses and attempt to conquer them. Try to recall those moments when you were through crises:

Are you an adult now?

What have you learned from these experiences?

Have you had anyone point an individual flaw in your appearance?

Are you impatient or shy?

Are you afraid of changing?

Are you afraid from the fear of being in the dark?

Do you harbor grudges over being unable to get past the circumstances?

Do you find it difficult to be open to criticism without becoming too cynical?

Mirror I hold a mirror...

The time is now for some reflection on yourself. Take a close look at the weaknesses you've previously identified:

Have you ever attempted to repair them?

What did you do to resolve the issues in your life?

Are you able to deal with the flaws of your character?

Opportunities = Weakness?

In the next step, you should carefully read what the description of your position says. Consider how you could connect your shortcomings to the description of the job. If you are able to determine the fact that you're "working on" similar problems that match the requirements of the interviewer, then you've found an agreement.

An example

"I prefer to concentrate on my strengths, rather than be concerned about my weaknesses. Like everyone else I'm still a work-in-progress. One thing I'm trying to master is patience. I am aware that I need patience with people particularly when I've created unrealistic expectations or expectations regarding their performance. However, since I am aware that I'm prone being impatient I rely on the knowledge and guidance of carefully selected advisers (or teammates) who will keep me on track."

What is this response saying? It indicates that I'm insisting. It states that I am aware that I can put high standards for other people. It also states that I could be prone to harsh judgments when these expectations aren't achieved. However, it also states that I'm aware of this part of myself, and I count on my team to help me balance my load. For me, this is a trait I appreciate in other people!

Another illustration

Here's a different method to answer the question: What's your biggest weakness? It's delegating:

"I have always felt it difficult to divide a job with others because I've always believed that I was capable of doing everything on my own. In the past, I considered soliciting help as an indication of insecurity. This is why I was able to take on a few tasks that have engulfed me that resulted in excessive frustration and anger. It was not an easy experience for me. But, I've begun to share the responsibility and tasks with other people. As a result I've been able get some incredible outcomes."

Pro Tip: Don't over-share!

Don't be timid! Don't lie about your flaws. Honesty, modesty and honesty are all admirable and good traits. However, ensure that the flaw you're trying to discover is easily rectified! Do not commit suicide in the workplace by acknowledging a grave fatal flaw. You're seeking a job and not their love!

Chapter 5: The Reasons Companies conduct Group Interviews

Since a few years now, reality television shows have been a regular feature on our television screens. The shows have attempted to meet each of our needs as viewers. Talent search shows on dancing, singing and general performance have paved the way for the careers of numerous famous artists of the present. Additionally, there are shows that attempt to create the mundane situations seem like they are part typical of our life. Reality shows that focus on celebrities through their day-to-day lives with love, finding love, and teenage pregnancies are some examples. Strategies games on reality television shows are also well-known. In these games, contestants are required to beat others to avoid be kicked out. The longer they stay in these types of game puts contestants close to the top prize.

Both Big Brother and the Survivor franchises are excellent examples of this.

Survival is an integral element of our life. If I could say it in the form of an old song that we "fight each day to stay free". Fighting isn't always bad but sometimes it's required to set oneself free or improve something. The work of Charles Darwin's Survival of the Fittest may be the most illustrative example of this. The constant evolution of animals has allowed them to develop advanced features that enable them to endure and pass on something to the next generation. It's a simple concept: either adapt or die. Simple as that.

This is also true in the job market. Candidates battle, outwit and beat each other out to get the job. In most cases the contest is conducted by a group of people who aren't aware of the performance of their rivals. This makes it difficult for contestants to discern who's taking the lead in the race.

The times have changed and hiring processes changed too. Interviews with individuals face-to-face now have another option that is called a group interview. This type of interview is designed to cut down on time as company presentations and interviews of multiple candidates are conducted simultaneously. Group job interviews are an excellent tool for employers to observe the behavior of applicants and how they interact with each other which is a crucial element in making teams that are successful. Work-related exercises, such as simulations and tasks are also part of the interview process. Interviewers also want to know who among the candidates are well-rounded. This refers to people who are able to work in a team and have a solid technical background yet are competent in working with other people. In the group interview, recruiters look at the appearance as well as the presentation, communication and presentation skills as well as the interest level of each applicant. Keep in the loop through the entire procedure. It doesn't matter whether you like it or not, getting called for an interview in a group is a dangerous game. You need to beat and beat every applicant in order to get the job. Only the best candidates will be able to be selected.

How to Ace Group Interviews

If you're reading the chapter before you may find your knees shaking at the idea of group interviews. Don't worry - it will not help at all. Keep calm and mentally prepare yourself into this one of unique challenge that you'll face. Remember that we mentioned earlier, it's the brain that runs every aspect of your life. Keep repeating this mantra repeatedly "If you think of it, then you will attain it. If you think about it, you will achieve it":

What are you wasting time to do? Prepare yourself for the group interview that you're scheduled to take part in. Here are some tips to be aware of to be the most fit candidate for the group.

Make sure you greet interviewers in turn. Make sure to look them in the eye as you introduce yourself and shake hands with firm force.

Make sure you arrive 10 minutes before the time of the interview to ensure you feel comfortable. Being the first to show up is not a good idea when you don't have any knowledge of the company or the job you're applying for. Always bring research , as well as physical copies of resumes as well as other documents.

Save your solution cheat sheets after you have arrived at the location. Sit comfortably and make a point of reviewing your notes without needing to glance at them.

There's no harm creating a two-minute introduction. Include in your introduction your education background, goals for your career as well as how this job fits you in terms of your abilities and experiences.

Do not waste your time on the toughest competitors in your group. Try to be engaging with each member in you are asking or answering questions to show team spirit.

Always remain calm by putting on a poker face. Do not display your shock or anger when you are in the group as it could get used against you by a smart monkey against you.

Learn to answer interview questions by looking up common interview questions and then taking the time to answer these questions. This will allow you to avoid lengthy pauses and mental blockages.

Being a wallflower, as usual, will get you nowhere. Be the leader among other candidates if you're being interviewed with them But remember that only mothers can the ability to know everything. Don't forget to make connections and acknowledge other candidates.

Be careful, but remain at peace. Keep in mind that your leadership abilities and ability to manage stress and pressure , as and teamwork skills are being scrutinized. Be aware before you act and put your top foot on the ground throughout the day.

Courtesy is the most important thing. Be sure to thank all interviewers following the interview process. Bonus points are awarded to those who recall the names and titles of the personnel as they say goodbye, or to write thank-you cards.

It's not too hard If you're prepared. Beyond physical preparations, it is important to prepare the mind and body to remain flexible and as fluid as sponge. It is impossible to guarantee anything in the world of life. If you've done all you could from the time you began to prepare until you wrote that thank you note, you don't have anything to be worried about. However, if you do not get that job, perhaps it wasn't the right fit for you.

More opportunities that fit you will be offered So, just stay patient and focus on making yourself the perfect candidate for every interview.

Face to Face Interviewing Basics of Interviewing Face To Face

As of now, I'm sure you've realized just how crucial and useful preparations are for major events. Interviews with job candidates play an essential part in the hiring process of a business. The process of conducting these interviews doesn't just aim at getting to know the applicant but they also serve to determine the skills of the candidate and the suitability of an individual with the group or to the company.

Doing your best to cheat through the process of preparing for your job interview is harmful to everyone else except you. For help in preparing Here are 15 essential points to keep in mind in your face-to-face job interview.

1. Be there earlier than the time you are scheduled to allow yourself to relax and get acquainted with the workplace.
2. Be sure to announce your arrival by asking the receptionist to confirm your arrival. It is likely that she will note the time of your entry and give you points to early bird.
3. Be aware regarding your own hygiene as well as your attire to make sure you create a positive impression.
4. Make sure your handshakes are firm and clear to show your sincerity.
5. Make sure you are confident in your body throughout the day, even when you're anxious. This will give you the confidence you need also make a lasting impression.
6. Before you take the interview, ensure that you've collected enough details about the company as well as the job you're seeking.
7. Remember that you sell yourself to prospective employers. It is not necessary

to be proud of your accomplishments, however, you should try to portray yourself as someone who can be able to make a positive change to the business.

8. Inquiring intelligently about the company or the topics that have been discussed in the interview to demonstrate that you're truly keen. The preparation of a set of questions based upon your previous research is equally acceptable.

9. Be prepared to answer commonly asked questions beforehand to ensure you don't get taken by surprise. Doing interviews with your family or friends can assist you in preparing for the big day.

10. Relax, relax, relax! In the daytime or just a few hours prior to your interview, put down your notes and fill your mind with positive thoughts to keep an optimistic outlook.

11. Don't forget any collateral that you might require during the interview like your resume or portfolio. Always keep a

basic colored marker and an aprons on for the event of.

12. Make sure you keep your phone away from other gadgets and small objects that could distract interviewers by their noise.

13. Honesty is the most effective policy. Do not try to create tales and explanations for things you don't understand since it can make you appear like a fool. But talking about things you don't understand will make you appear at ease and curious.

14. Make sure you are professional. Interviews for jobs are not an actual TV show in which you can share your deepest emotions. Be sure to keep your answers short and succinct in order to respect the time both you and the interviewer took.

15. When you leave, be sure to thank you and make it clear that you want to get the job you think about it. Don't be afraid to express your thoughts, but do not over-exaggerate it.

Chapter 6: Questions to Test Commitment and Motivation

People are often chosen based on their skills alone. This is a major mistake.

I've made a lot of hiring mistakes , by searching for skills that can be used in the job, and limiting my interview strictly to what needs to be accomplished by the applicant within the next 6-12 months. The candidates would have amazing experience and enough skills to complete the job that needs to be completed today. The hiring process is so appealing because you can see that they'll instantly relieve some of the pain.

Most of the time when the world is changing in their direction, people are stuck. They are not able to adapt quickly. The most desirable employees are those who are able to be successful in the present, but also be able to learn and adjust.

It is much more likely to recruit an outstanding person when you ask questions that reveal how they think and hire innovative people who are quick to learn. Therefore, use the questions below to determine the capacity of the individual has to grow and determine how quickly they'll grow. The people who have the greatest potential for growth and fastest speed (smarts and determination) are the best candidates to hire.

This method is useful for hiring summer interns to the top executives. I've used this approach at all levels, when I discovered that sticking to the specifications of the job may not always work.

There's a huge difference in the ability to deal with the smoothness that each job requires. Think of those clock-watchers that you've encountered - those who put in the minimum amount of effort required to stay in their job, but not much more! The most important thing you don't want to do is to recruit more of them.

The questions in this section are a crucial element of your interview to allow you to probe more than the mere capability. You're looking for people who are truly driven

to get things done

to be able to function in a larger team

to learn continuously throughout their lives, ensuring that their abilities remain current.

Candidates who are weak will always be confused by the following questions. This is why they are excellent to identify those who give any thought about what they can do to improve their performance. Find out how they can help.

What is a successful career for you?

What do you think of your current progress in your job?

How successful do you think you to have been?

Where do you stand against your fellows?

What are you doing to be more effective in your job?

What did you do to improve yourself in the last year?

Which publications have you read that have had the biggest impact on your professional life?

What keeps you motivated?

What are some things that are difficult for you to accomplish?

What were your mistakes over the last year? and what have you learned from these mistakes?

What are the challenges you're looking for in your new job?

How often do you take time off sick?

How can you keep yourself engaged?

What have you learned in the past twelve months?

Where do you draw your inspiration?

People who consistently accomplish the goals they set out to achieve, who are constantly developing their skills, and clearly are motivated are the people you're looking for.

But don't dismiss those who have experienced setbacks those who have smashed into the roadblock in their lives multiple times and have overcome each time generally have plenty of motivation as well.

Personal organisation, and the ability to function under stress

Inability to efficiently manage their time or who break down when they feel pressure can be a major risk. There is no need for such people So don't just take the answers to these questions as if they were at their face worth.

Keep probing until you are convinced that the truth is beginning to emerge. Keep in mind that only a few people confess that they are unable or disorganized to perform under pressure in an interview.

How do you manage your time? controlling your schedule?

What value can you provide in your work?

What is success to you?

How do you prioritize your work when you're full of work?

How do you deal with the pressure of having many things to accomplish?

What kind of goals do you have for you?

How can you keep track of them?

How many projects are you able to manage at one time?

How do you manage and plan major projects?

How do you plan your schedule to manage your day-to-day tasks?

How do you manage your time for assignments, projects, and when are holidays?

How often do you go over and beyond your duty to finish your work?

Which was your most difficult circumstance you've ever faced? How did you feel, as well as how did handle it?

Consider a time when things went off the rails. What did you do?

What are you planning to do with your day?

I want to know what planning system you employ and walk me through the process.

Do you have a story to share about a time where your performance didn't meet your expectations?

People who are able to clearly finish a task within the timeframe and under stress, are the ones to keep.

Businesses need employees who aren't afraid of work and that can be relied upon to complete the task in a timely manner and who don't require frequent reminders or constant supervision. These are the people who are aware of what has to be done and how to do it. It's as easy as that. So, snap the opportunity to meet them.

Concerns about the working style of employees and management

Emotional intelligence is an enormous difference, and people who have high levels of emotional intelligence are the ones you should hire. They have the following characteristics and are successful almost anywhere.

There is no need for people who complain and cause difficulties in their businesses since it's exhausting for everyone else around them. Thus, someone who is capable and willing, however unmanageable isn't the best choice.

Pay attention to the responses to the questions below can help you identify employees who behave as if they are old and not the size of their shoes. It can also help you get the ability to judge how their performance and behavior will positively impact your business, your clients and colleagues.

Why is this important? You can train employees on how to work and you can also refresh their abilities however, you are not able to guide, instruct or guide people to maintain a an attitude of positivity.

If you were promoted What is the most likely motive?

If you were fired, what is the most likely reasons?

What have you received the most often criticised and who did it? Why?

What do your bosses, coworkers and colleagues describe you? Why?

What are your working habits? How do they alter when your boss is not there?

How do you manage while you're left to your own devices?

Write about the most successful manager you've ever worked with.

What was it that made them stand out? And what was it that you loved about them?

What was the last time you were angry at your job? What was the reason?

Imagine a time in your life where people who were around you weren't as direct or honest as they could be. What did you do? How would you like to be handled?

What is your boss's reaction when you leave and how do you deal with it?

What kind of rewards feel the most satisfying to you?

What do you think your dream work day be like?

Be aware that people who always believe that another person is to blame for their issues (never them) or those who never feel satisfied, or have negative or "I don't care" attitude are not good news. Don't hire them.

Chapter 7: Spreading the Word - Feel The Power of Affirmations and Subliminals

What would be great to have a system that, once you've set it up, requires minimal effort, effort or money to assist you in learning to increase your confidence and abilities to perform well in interviews?

Here's a straightforward but extremely effective way to utilize your goals, as well as those new ideas you'd like take on - and to do just this.

* Reading Your Words

This simple technique that is often overlooked it's almost absurd to label it a "technique that is to go through lists of objectives and fresh convictions on a daily basis. If you are able to perform this at least twice per every day, then that's fantastic. Also, If you have somewhere safe to read your statements out loud , all the better. These will eventually be referred to as affirmations. The simple act of reading through your new goals and convictions will, over time, be sufficient alone to bring about the changes you desire because your mind will gradually accept every statement as true.

For faster, more effective and convenient results , you must hear the same statements frequently. They reach a higher level of your brain rather than just reading them to yourself. The more you are able to hear them and the more you think about them, the more your brain will take in the ideas.

* Listening to Your Words

The most effective way to accomplish this is to tape yourself saying your purpose and your beliefs out loud. Set the recording to loop (repeat repeatedly) for at least 30 minutes. You should repeat this whenever you want throughout the entire day.

It's possible to do this using the voice recorder application on your tablet or smartphone or any other device that is easy to use and listen whenever you have some free time. It's possible to go to sleep in the night by while listening to them. This actually makes for a great time to do and is a great method to gain access to the deepest levels of your mind , as you'll discover in the next section.

* Putting Your Words to Music

To take this basic voice recording technique to the next step (which I personally prefer) that I prefer personally) you can apply some music backing the recording.

Don't think you're supposed to singing the words, or sing them, unless you're really interested! You can simply embed your spoken vocal track on a music source. A track that is peaceful and relaxing to listen is ideal. The benefit of this more musical approach can be that it doesn't need to be able to hear your voice within the mix to make it be effective. The reason is that the words are recognized at a subconscious level, and thus be efficient in reprogramming your brain subliminally.

When I make recordings of my own affirmations I turn the volume of my vocal to a low level within the recording. The idea is that I could barely discern any phrase or word over the whole album of calming instrumental music that I loop the vocal on.

One important thing to remember one thing to remember is the less you mix the vocals, then the easier it is to utilize the whole recording when there are others in the vicinity and they aren't wondering what that you're hearing!

Whatever way you decide to go about it, putting your voice to music will mean you will be able to listen to the music you love and also reap the benefits of the affirmations that are leaking into your brain, slowly creating confidence in your interview skills and helping you get closer to your goals.

If you decide to make use of music, you'll require some basic multi-track software , assuming that you don't have one already. I still use a few that I purchased for music mixing on a PC (Sony Acid) however, there are free alternatives like Audacity, among others that which you can download through the app store on your smartphone or tablet.

Utilize your recordings daily and at every opportunity. For instance, in the gym, while working, studying at home, laying down to sleep (as previously mentioned) relaxation, general reading , or even on the road (one of my personal favorites). Make sure you spend at least an hour every time to give your brain the most opportunity to absorb all the details.

It doesn't matter if you choose to make the basic voice recording, or transform it into something that is more musical, after you've made it, all that's needed to make use of this method is to switch on the device you're planning to listen to. You don't need to concentrate on the words or paying attention while the recording plays. The positive messages that are being presented will continue to be absorbed and soon will be accepted by the brain as truth.

* Invisible Programming: Sending Subliminal Success Messages to Youself

The reason that I choose to put my recorded affirmations in music in a way that I am unable to constantly discern the words over the background music is due to what's known as "subliminal" messages. These are those that are communicated by a secret or disguised manner, and are below the boundaries of your consciousness. They are able to escape your conscious mind and go straight into the subconscious mind. This makes them particularly useful in their role as an added tool in shaping your beliefs and thoughts.

There's a different method to subliminally communicate to change your beliefs , and that is by listening instead of seeing. It's possible to do this making use of pre-made software or applications for your tablet, PC or mobile phone.

This is what I consider to be the most effective subliminal messaging program for computers available - Silent Ideas. It's an excellent tool with many years study behind it (and there's no way I'm connected to the company). You can try out for free the numerous ready-made subliminal messages for various areas of your life and then, if you like it, buy the full version where you can insert unlimited amounts your own new interview/job-hunting beliefs.

There are applications available on iTunes however, since I'm not a user, I can't myself recommend any. I do however recommend Subliminal Messages Pro by Megabit which is available for Android through Google Play. There's an "Lite" version that's free as well as the "Pro" version that's affordable. Both aren't as advanced than Silent Ideas but still great even when you're on the move.

You can type the written affirmations you made in the previous software, and the messages will flashed at you every day when you use the device.

It's impossible to read them consciously, so they won't disrupt what else you're doing with the device. However, they'll start to influence you at an emotional scale. When you keep exposing yourself to these messages that are subliminal about the "new you" and you'll begin to notice that every step you take towards reaching your goal is easier and lasts longer.

Similar to the other strategies described in this section, slowly you'll begin to act and act as if someone has a completely different inner dialogue as an interviewee or job candidate than you've accustomed to.

It is possible that you feel you are compelled to find more or more challenging jobs and send out your resume more frequently and even begin to relish the once-stressful interview situations.

You now know how to increase your confidence in yourself by using your written and spoken words, let's discuss how you can practice to improve your presentation techniques and succeed through images and pictures!

Chapter 8: Before The Interview

Study the Company & Industry

If there's something that drives me mad during my interviews with candidates it's when they fail to conduct any thorough research on the industry or company. There is no need to know the background of the company since its beginning or even look at its website to get an idea the structure of it, its locations and the way it earns money. If it's a publicly traded firm, you will find an abundance of data in its SEC documents that can be found online.

Find out if you're an ideal fit with the culture of a company is among the most crucial factors when getting the right job. On a company's site you'll often see its missionstatement, values as well as its successes and distinctive features of its company's culture. Once you have done some research on these elements, you might decide to not take a company out of an interview if it doesn't appear to be an ideal match. For instance, if a company's goal is to increase recycling worldwide by 75% but you're not really interested in recycling, you may want to consider other possibilities. There's an old but true expression in the business world where people accept jobs to make money, but they leave due to the company's culture.

If you're considering changing industries, you should do some research about the industry you are targeting. What laws regulate it? Who are the major players? What are the main competitors to the company you want to target? Which firms are established and which ones are emerging? What is the direction of the industry? What is the best way to leverage technology?

The ability to talk about the factors mentioned above during an interview will distinguish you from the other applicants. If you're having a difficult time finding any of the information you need, write an agenda of questions and bring it along with on the day of the interview. Make sure to ask intelligent questions and listen to the responses making notes. If the interviewer isn't certain of how to answer your query, don't press, simply leave it out and move on to the next question.

Google the interviewer

The interviewer holds your resume on their desk however, what are you aware of the person you're interviewing? You're likely to have an LinkedIn account, or some other information about their professional life online. What is the length of time they've worked in the business? Which companies did they work with before? What causes are they involved with? I'm not suggesting you follow your interviewer but it's useful to collect a little details about them, especially when you're thinking of topics to discuss. The information can be integrated into conversations at different occasions and impress interviewers with your abilities to do the necessary research.

I've seen a candidate (during an interview panel) disseminated all the LinkedIn profiles of every panel member on the table when the interview began. She had more questions to ask regarding our qualifications and backgrounds than we did about her! In the beginning I was not sure whether I was pleased or scared by her findings. We ultimately were impressed and eventually hired her.

Make sure you know your resume

Prepare to talk about each bullet section of your resume, which includes your previous work experiences. Interviewers was once asking me about my experience at an earlier job that was 8 years prior to my current job. It is impossible to predict what an interviewer will be focusing on, so be sure to think about your entire professional career and have a list of examples prepared for each bullet point.

Changes in employment are another subject that interviewers frequently examine. It is crucial to talk about the changes to your job in a positive manner even if there were negative factors that led to your termination. If you've been fired and you were not told the truth about the reason for it. In the interview, you should say that it was not a good fit , and the company was able to let you go. If you've been laid off, it is more straightforward to describe.

If you quit one company for another and are asked to explain what you think made the new job more appropriate. Was it able to offer you a significant raise? An opportunity to expand your career? An opportunity to try something novel? Management that is more accommodating?

Bring Copies of your Resume

You will be meeting lots of people at your office and some of them might have been sent your resume electronically, but did not bring it with them when it's time to speak to you. Five copies of your resume in case of need will solve this issue. Begin in asking interviewers if they've got an original copy of your resume. If not, give them one.

Bring a notebook and pen to take notes. It is not recommended that cell phones or electronic devices are suitable to take notes since these devices could give the interviewer the impression you're easily distracted. It is important to keep eye contact and taking short notes.

Critique Yourself

Examine the job description carefully and then compare it with your resume. Where are the gaps? What are the skills you lack? It is likely that the interviewer will want you to fill in the areas. Make sure you can explain how other abilities you possess fill in the gaps you don't. This is especially crucial in the event that you're changing to a completely new industry. Take note of your abilities that are applicable to the new field and highlight your skills during the interview.

The company I was employed by had a rotation system for engineers. They could go throughout the department of audit and gain knowledge about the other departments of the business. One engineer I talked to was a master at explaining the importance of being detail-oriented in engineering be, and how this could be very beneficial in auditing. She was offered the job!

Be Positive

You must be in a positive attitude and in a positive mood prior to the interview. Just a few hours prior to the interview, you can listen to some of your favourite music, check out funny YouTube video clips, or talk to your friend. Any thing you could do to ease anxiety and set the mind at ease prior to the interview is highly recommended. It is important to present your best you and radiate positive energy. A cheerful and positive candidate makes the task of interviewers easier and improves your chances of securing an offer.

Conduct mock interviews

Do you have certain questions in interviews that you are afraid to answer? What about "where do you imagine yourself five years from now? That question should be removed in the last five years! Create a list of the possible questions that you'd like to be asked (including those that you've never heard of) and then ask a friend or relative to take on the role of interviewer as you play. Record or videotape the practice session for more information. You can practice responding to the exact question six to eight times until your answer feels natural and comfortable. Ask the interviewer you mocked to provide their feedback after the interview has ended. Make notes and schedule another session of practice if needed. The more you practice relaxed, the better prepared you'll be in your interview.

Below are some common questions you can be prepared for:

"Tell me about your self."

"What did you do that made you interested in this job?"

"Where do you want to be in five years' time?"

"Do your prefer to work on your own or in an organization?"

"Do you enjoy being in charge of people?"

"Have you conducted any research about your company?"

"What is it that you are passionate about?"

"What do you see as your short- and long-term goals for your career?"

"What is your strongest and your weaknesses?"

"What is your expectations regarding the salary?"

To find more questions that are great as well as some tips on how to respond go to this website.

Think Like an Interviewer

The job of an interviewer is to determine your capabilities and talents as well as your personal characteristics to determine if you're the right match for the company or department. That's it! Once you have a clear idea of the things they're looking for Think about the way you'll present the item to them. The interviewer will ask questions about the areas below (I have included similar questions to aid you in your preparation):

* Strengths: Does your job require written or verbal communication? Selling? Thinking critically? explaining technical terms? Review the job description carefully and compare your strengths and experience to the bullet points that are relevant.

* Work Ethics Do you make yourself work extra hours when it is necessary? Do you make yourself accountable for deadlines and projects? Do you have the ability to work on your own, without having a boss hounding you?

*Leadership: Have your been able to lead others? What is your management style? Can you motivate your direct reports?

* Flexibility How do you manage the effects of change? Stress? Tight deadlines? People who are difficult? Do you know how to master new skills with little effort?

Contributions: In your previous posts (work or volunteering) What positive changes brought you? What did the figures or any other metrics for operations change under your supervision? What is your supervisor's view of your performance in the context of these metrics? What projects did you get given and what did you get out of them?

• Creativity. Are imaginative when it comes down to solving issues? Are you able to think about problems from a different perspective or from a different perspective? Bring a few specific examples for the interview.

Dress to be Successful

As a fervent believer, I think in the fact that both male and female applicants are expected to dress professionally for interviews. That is, business attire (with tie) for males and formal attire for women. Make sure your suit is professionally dry-cleaned prior every interview, and make sure that it's free of pet hair prior to leaving the door. Your shoes should be shiny. The color are supposed to be muted and dark but not loud or loud.

There are a few certain exceptions to the dress code. For instance, if you are interviewing for tech companies within Silicon Valley, suits are generally considered inappropriate, so dress wearing something less formal (maybe not wearing a jacket). If you are in this situation, inquire to inquire about the appropriate dress code is for potential candidates. The first thing that an interviewer is looking at is how you're dressed. If you don't dress appropriately your attire, the interview may get worse from there. Do not leave anything up to chance with regards to the attire you wear for interviews Think of it as an investment when you are forced to pay for a few dollars to upgrade them.

Don't wear perfume or cologne during an interview. It can be distracting for the interviewer, as there's no good reason for you to risk that.

Get Your References Prepared

If the company is serious in hiring you, generally they'll ask for references once the interview is completed but it's still recommended to have a list of references in place prior to the interview to be prepared in case. Choose 3-5 individuals and notify them in advance to ensure they're willing to act as an example. You must ensure they're competent and willing to testify to your qualifications and work experience. If you are applying for your first job outside of school, then you should consider academic advisers or expert mentors. List your references , including their name address, phone number, email and when you collaborated with them. Keep your references list in order and only supply it upon request. If you do get the job take the time to send an acknowledgement email to all references who were approached.

Start Before the Time!

It isn't a good idea to be anxious about transportation and be late (or just in time) to your interview. Doing a run-through on a different day could be beneficial, if possible. It is recommended to arrive 15 minutes before the scheduled time for the bathroom to get settled, then gather your thoughts. It is also utilized to look around and gather information regarding the working environment and the work environment. If there's lots of screaming and people are moving around like crazy it's not an appropriate indicator.

Treat everyone with respect

The interview doesn't start until you're in the office. It begins from the moment you leave the front door. Try to smile and show respect to everyone. This includes parking lot attendants as well as receptionists at the location you are interviewing at. While they may not be an integral part of the interview, they might be required to give an evaluation to interviewers regarding your conduct prior to or following the interview. If you did well in the interview but behaved rudely to the receptionist just before it began, more than likely, you'll be taken off the list.

It is possible that unexpected things happen. Perhaps you were validated for parking, but when you attempted to leave the garage for parking the garage, it did not work. now you must pay the price of $12. Don't be upset and head back to the garage. Simply pay the fine and walk out. This isn't worth all the stress it could cause, particularly when the interview went without a hitch.

Chapter 9: The Cover Letter

Many people worry about cover letters. They aren't as difficult as they are made out to be. The cover letter you write should that is short and concise. It is essential to make sure that it is addressed to the person who is in charge of hiring.

Cover letters are intended to give the employer an incentive to read the resume. Like the resume it is essential for the cover letter to appear free of spelling and grammar mistakes.

The Structure of the Letter

Start with a an appropriate, formal greeting. Make it clear what job you're applying to so that there is no guesswork for the person who is recruiting you. It should not be more than two or three sentences in length.

In the next paragraph, you should let the recruiter know why it is that you have applied for the position and would like to work for them. In this section, you could emphasize your prior experience or explain for things that aren't listed or unclear on your resume.

It is important to conclude with the desire to hear back from the person you are thanking the person for taking time. It should be brief and courteous, leaving an appropriate message to the person who is recruiting.

If you adhere to this format and follow this structure, you'll always have a well-written cover letter that's not annoying to a prospective employer and lets them make quick decisions about your resume.

Interview Questions

Questions get difficult. There are some common questions interviewers are asked, but there are others which are only for recent graduates of colleges and others that are not permitted to ask. There are some that you must be asking. We will help you become aware of some of these questions.

Common Questions

Many of them are routine and are frequently asked by interviewers.

1. Can you share something about you? (Make the statement positive)
2. How do you deal with stressful or challenging situations?
3. How do you respond to criticism?
4. How do you define success?
5. Why do you believe you'd be a good match for this company? (Research is helpful here)
6. Have had the experience of being dismissed? Why?
7. Where do you envision your self in the next five years? Ten?
8. Do you prefer working either as a soloist or in a team?
9. Why do you wish to work for this company?
10. How do you deal with differing points opinions with your co-workers or supervisors?
11. Why should I choose you?

Recent Graduate-related Questions

There are certain questions that are likely to be asked of you if you're newly graduated from college.

1. What is your top memorable college experience?
2. What was your extracurricular activity?
3. How can you put into practice what you learned in your college classes to this job?
4. What did you do to prepare yourself for college to work-life to make the transition?
5. Are you planning to attend graduate school? If yes, do you plan to be working as well?
6. What kind of hands-on experience did you gain during your time at college?
7. How do you feel that college has prepared you for the job you are currently working in?
8. What did you do for an internship?
9. What are you thinking you can be able to bring to the company?

Questions that employers cannot ask

There are certain kinds of questions that are not or are not legal to ask. A lot of people do not realise that they should not be asked.

1. Anything related to the age.

2. Any questions regarding children, marital status and child care plans sexual preferences, etc.

3. Personal health questions.

4. Questions about ethnicity.

5. Anything related to disabilities.

6. Arrest records. They will only request information for information if you've been convicted of a crime. There are no other information.

7. Any other personal information is not allowed.

Your Questions

There are some questions you'll want to know the answers to which are suitable to inquire about.

1. Why do you think this job is available?

2. How many times was this position filled in the last five years?

3.What could this new employee differ from the previous employee?

4.What do you want to see happen over the next six months?

5.What are the biggest challenges in this job?

6.What is my level of autonomy in my decision-making?

7.What are the options for advancement?

8.Has the company been successful before?

9.What are the most significant changes you expect to see for the business in the near term?

10.What can make a person succeed in their job?

Chapter 10: The Interview Process

The job interview or sales meeting will kick off an process that can have three possible outcomes: You'll be either selected for the job or receive a notification that they've hired another person or receive no message in any way. The process is not just left to chance. So, you should prepare in advance what you'll do during your entire meeting to demonstrate that you are not just more desirable than others, but also that you have greater to offer than what you are able to offer in terms of payment. Also, you must demonstrate the fact that you possess more to offer than the other candidates also competing for the job. If you follow the guidelines in the chapter you'll be able to communicate your worth during an interview in that it creates an irresistible chance for you to be hired.

The process of interviewing is broken into five steps:

*The Introduction
*Information Sharing
*Information Gathering
*The Closing
*Follow-up

The remainder part of the chapter dedicated to explaining each step.

The Introduction

In the majority of cases, at the start of an interview the first question is usually "Can you share something about your background?" When asking this question, employers aren't expecting to know every single one of your life or professional experiences since your birth. They're asking you to prove that you're the best candidate to be hired. This is your chance to establish an example for them for the remainder in the meeting by sharing your story. The ability to tell your story lets you to present your personal life in a way which answers the three questions:

1. What are you doing now?

2. Why are you interested in this position ? And why should you do it now?

3. Why should we choose you?

While these questions appear easy in their answers, lots of struggle or stumble with the final one. I've met several professionals who believe that claiming you're dedicated, team-oriented or a dedicated professional etc. suffices to be able to answer this question in depth. A majority of the descriptions are, however, subjective and do not allow employers to gauge your performance. Employers want to know what you've done in the past, so that they can assess what you could be able of doing for them in the near future. They don't hire you by your potential, they hire you based on your achievements. Use your three most notable achievements from chapter 3 to create your narrative.

Your story should be written with this structure

1. The "Beginning" The "Beginning" is the place where you went to school or began your career.

2. Your passion The reason for this is what prompted you to begin your current job.

3. Your achievements Your Achievements - These are the relevant previous achievements that the employer would like to hear about.

4. The Reason You're Here Today Your answer will be based on the way you answer your sentence in the next sentence * "I'm here to interview today due to ....."

5. The Future You Want to See - This's the place where you talk about your future goals and explain how working at this company can get you toward them.

If you're able to tell your story for longer than two minutes, you might notice that the interviewer isn't taking note of the information you're sharing. Be sure to keep it short and direct. Create your story ahead of time Practice it with your people you know and find ways to keep it short and succinct while explaining your worth.

Information Distribution

Many job seekers find that the most challenging aspect of preparation for the interview process is to be prepared to respond to every question that is asked. In a job market that is competitive employers aren't just trying to determine whether you're the most qualified candidate but they also want for tough questions that could make you unqualified for the interview process and help them in their job. The most crucial mindset to use when answering these types of questions is to make sure that you think of it as an exercise. The process of interviewing is a contest to decide who will demonstrate themselves in the most effective way to impress the employer. Thinking of the procedure as a game allows you to increase your creativity in deciding the way you'll play every question to be asked.

In general, there are only five questions you'll be asked in the interview. These are:

1. Why would you like to work for us?

In answering this question, you need to think about how working at this business will be a part of your career plans for the long term. It is also important to consider what you actually enjoy about the company.

2. What is the advantage from having you work for our firm?

If you've completed all the exercises in chapter three, you'll be capable of answering the question by discussing the things you've accomplished in the past, and then how you can attain similar or even greater results for their business.

3. What kind of person are you?

Employers will inquire about four different forms to answer this query. They want to know whether you're easily able to work with and if you can be a part of the culture of the company. The first type is an interview question that begins with the words, "Tell me about a moment that you ...." could cite your previous accomplishments and employ the SOAR technique (explained in chapter 3) to discuss the scenario that you were in, the challenges you had to overcome and the steps you took through and the outcomes you achieved to answer the question in a concise manner.

The other form of this question is to inquire about your weak points. This is a response to the fear that you may have a serious personality flaw that prevents you from doing a good job in your job. It's easy to answer by not just highlighting an actual and fixable flaw however, you should also mention how you handled the issue before. You could also go a step further and show how your weaknesses are actually an advantage that allows you to stand out from others.

The third version of this question could be formulated in a variety of ways: What made you quit your current job? What was the relationship between you and your former boss? No matter if you were fired or reduced in size or quit, it is important to always be positive about your employer or boss, and present your departure as an opportunity you had actively searched for when you wanted for a long-term job opportunity.

The fourth type may be in the form of a reason for the some gaps on your resume. Respond to this question by talking about your consulting or volunteer work as well as your study at college to learn new abilities or in search of your purpose or career direction.

4. What distinguishes you from other candidates we are looking at for the same job?

When considering this question, take note of your unique approach that you have used to accomplish many of your achievements to this point. Your unique approach is what differentiates you from other applicants. Additionally, based on the research you conducted in chapter 3 Think about what your unique method and knowledge of the industry will assist employers solve their problems in a way that is superior to what any other candidate.

5. Do I have the money to pay for your services?

In the course of an interview, the employer might inquire about your salary specifications. The trick in this scenario is that if the requirements are excessive, they may not be interested in your application. However If your demands are not enough then you could be taking money off the table during negotiations. The perceived value that employers place on you could decrease if you're asking for less than what they anticipated to pay. The method you use for solving this issue is covered thoroughly in the chapter six.

Information getting

At the end during the conversation, your host will ask you if there are any concerns to ask the interviewer. In this moment, good questions are crucial to the success of your interview. There are many reasons to be asking good questions in this interview. These are the most important

* It will help you understand the challenges that employers face and the issues they'll require an experienced candidate to tackle.

The right questions can help you establish a an excellent rapport. This will to create a sense of security so that the interviewer can more easily divulge important information, allowing the user to tailor how they can utilize your individual service to suit their specific needs.

* It allows you to demonstrate that your skills are different from the other candidates.

Good questions can boost your credibility with employers as well as stimulate their minds and help them develop a positive perception about your personal service you offer.

It is not advisable to ask any question just for the purpose or asking questions. You should choose your questions cautiously. The criteria you choose to use to select the questions you ask are based on the factors that are crucial to you when starting a new position and what that you think is not in your knowledge of the requirements of the employer as well as the responsibilities associated with the job.

The method of asking questions starts by identifying areas in which you have no information regarding the position. Spend 15 minutes prior to your interview to conduct the following questions to help decide what questions you'll ask the interviewer:

Step 1. What should I know about what employers are looking for in a perfect candidate?

Who you talk to could make a difference, either negative or positive impact on your chances of being chosen or scheduled for the next phase during the selection process. Every interviewer will have an individual view of what the ideal candidate will be. Since the roles performed by your interviewers may vary consider whether you recognize the names and the background of every person you interview with. If you're not sure the names of those you interview, simply contact the person who organized the interview to inquire about the names of the people. They'll usually not be shy about giving you the names. When you are familiar with their full names and addresses, you can check the profiles of their on LinkedIn or perform the Google search for their names with quotes. Utilizing quotes allows you to search for their first and last names in a complete.

Try your self in their shoes Consider the expertise of each interviewer in relation to the job you're conducting an interview for. For instance, if you are interviewing for a sales position , and you are interviewing with someone in Sales, they has a different perspective on the way they would like marketing to help with sales for the business.

Step 2: What should I know to know about the position and its duties?

Think about how well you know the specific requirements for the job. Are you aware enough regarding the position to be able to clearly link it to your prior successes? What can you do to achieve similar, or better, in their organization?

Step 3. What should I know about the issues or difficulties that the employee hired be faced with?

Check to see if you know the kind of issues the new employee will need to deal with every day. Consider why these specific concerns are crucial for the employer.

Step 4: What should I know to learn about the organization it self and the work environment?

Think about the way in which the company's culture is compatible with your own personality. Do you know if your present environment is one that you are able to succeed?

After you have completed the four steps before Write down the details that are the most crucial to you. Consider what you'll use to frame your question in order to gather this information during your interview without receiving incomprehensible and confusing responses. Below, you'll see a few possible questions you could use. It is recommended at least three or five of these questions prepared in advance for every person that you interview.

What do you expect to see coming up for your business in the coming five years?

What do you consider to be your company's most valuable assets?

* What do you want to describe about your latest product or growth plans?

• What was the fate of the previous person to hold this position?

What were the main advantages and disadvantages of the prior person in this position?

* What kinds of abilities do you have that you don't have in your arsenal that you're trying to replace by bringing on a new employee?

What is the general organisational structure and how does your department fit into to the overall structure?

What are the career options within this department?

* What do you think as the top aspect of your job?

* What are the strengths and qualities you are most interested in when hiring someone for this job?

* Can you explain an average day or week in this job?

• What is the immediate problems facing the current situation that have to be addressed within the next three months?

- What is the expectations for performance for this job over the first twelve months?

Closing

Many people can be able to give a fantastic interview, however fail to wrap it up in a proper manner. It's like giving an unwrapped Christmas present and not wrapping it properly. After you have asked all the questions, you need to follow these five essential steps to increase your odds of being hired:

1. Thanks for your time and effort.

2. Discuss how you feel about the position and explain why you feel this way ("I'm attracted to the position because..."). ..."). Make sure to give three reasons for why you'd be the perfect candidate for this job.

3. You can ask: "Do you see me as a good fit to be in this job?" Be very sincere and direct in asking this question.

4. If they do not then ask them: "What are your major concern about my credentials?" Make sure you pay attention

without interrupting the interviewer. Collect all of the interviewer's arguments to the reason you may not be the right candidate to the job. Be prepared to respond to each objection by providing an explanation for to support the argument. The reason why it shouldn't be a problem with the hiring manager. You must conclude this section by asking "Have I addressed all of your questions about accepting this job?" If the answer is NO, inquire what the interviewer's remaining concerns are and then continue to discuss your concerns.

If yes If so, you can inquire "Where should we begin from this point?" Or, "What next?"

5. In this moment, a lot of people don't request the job. Some assume that since they're in the interview, it's already established that they are interested in the job. But, the majority of companies insist that you ask for the job in the course of the interview. You could mention one of:

"After all the things we talked about I'd want to consider being considered for this position. What do we do from this point?"
Or
"This job opportunity is in line with my career objectives, and I'm confident I'll be able to do a amazing task for your. Who are the other key decision making factors in deciding who gets selected for this job?"
It is important to speak with conviction and passion. Enthusiasm sells.

The Follow-up

After your interview, you should send a follow-up note at night or on the day following it. The earlier you send it more quickly, the more effective. Most job applicants write this letter to express their gratitude to you for the chance to be interviewed by an organization. However, the mentality of a salesperson demands you to take a step further to increase the probability of getting invited to the next phase in the process of interviewing. This kind of follow-up letter can be used as an tool to influence the company's decision to invite you back for a follow-up interview. It's also a chance to elaborate and justify any reason why the company may not be interested in hiring you. In writing this letter, it is important to consider four things:

1. In comparison to my competitors who are my competitors, what could be the top two reasons they have for not hiring me?

2. What were some of the most important concerns that interviewers expressed about my qualifications to be hired during the interview?

3. What are the top three reasons why employers should choose to hire me?

4. What solutions do I could use to assist in solving some of the issues the interviewer faces within their department?

The follow-up letter you send should be the following format:

A Four- or Five-Paragraph Essay

*The Opening:

Please thank them for having interviewed you.

Summary of your background and reasons why they should employ you:

* Three or two sentences.

Two or three paragraphs that address their concern(s) regarding hiring you or sharing the problem-solving ideas you've got for your department

*Ending: What you'd like for them to accomplish:

* Ask to speak with them more regarding your ideas if you have shared your ideas.

* Be clear about why you are interested in to be hired:

The interviewer won't just take this for granted;

The way to do this is by telling the interviewer, "I would like to be thought of for the next stage of the interviewing process" as well as "I am interested in being considered to do this position."

Chapter 11: What to Discuss

Okay. Everyone gets nervous. Breathe deeply and exhale by letting your nostrils open. Begin doing this prior to when you begin your interview. If you're uncontrollably anxious, think of a memory of someone you cherish that will help create peace. A brief prayer works well. Whatever method you decide to use to calm yourself, keep doing it until your nervousness eases that is when it's going to happen. Interviewers are just like us. If they were nervous, interviewers are likely to prefer doing something else.

When you're at the table with any interviewers, keep in mind that they might think that you're competent for the job by reading your resume. Therefore, when you realize this you can relax. Consider your responses and answers for a few seconds. Be careful not to hurl your responses. Instead, take your time and then elaborate. It's impressive to me whenever a candidate has the time to consider the answer. This tells me they think about things.

I am always interested in asking applicants why they are searching for the job. The answer usually reveals something about their personality such as: I'm looking to earn more money. I would like to grow. I would like to spend to spend more time with my children. I would like to improve my knowledge. These are great solutions. Who wouldn't want these things? The interviewers themselves would like these items too!

When you're asked to answer a question about the reasons you're looking for a job, you should be mindful not to discuss your negative feelings about people, specifically concerning your boss or the company you work for or for. If an interviewer wants to know more in a question like this you might want to say something like "it's an excellent job but I'm not sure that I have the right opportunity" or something similar.

There's a good chance that you'll have negative thoughts about your boss, or the company but don't erase yourself because you've just proved your whining. Or that you're not able to get along with your colleagues. I've had a lady say to me that her boss is a snob. It could be true however she could have come up with an argument that said "I'm in no way learning, and need to get my feet wet". What's the difference?

The other thing you must keep in mind is to address every person present during the interview. There are companies that conduct panel interviews that may involve individuals from the departments which you'll interact with. They could be supervisors or employees who have a say in the hiring process. These companies are aware of the importance of selecting the right candidate and are seeking an ideal fit across the board.

If there are several interviewers, you are sure that they will all be going through your interview to assess your performance. Even if just one of them is the one to ask questions or conducts the interview, be sure to consider and include all the participants in the room when you answer. As an interviewer someone doesn't pay attention to me and only addresses his questions to only one person, I feel a bit secluded and can be annoyed. You should be consistently watching the table in front of every person in your answers. It is telling the story of who is you and the way you be a part of their success. Be sure that everyone is aware of this fantastic story!

Chapter 12: What is the reason Finding A Job is important?

A job is described as work that does doesn't just keep a person engaged but also allows him to achieve economic compensation. In this decade, the financial aspect has become increasingly more important and, without it the description has no significance. What was once a job on the farm of your father to grow paddy has been replaced by working on an agricultural tractor for a contract farmer who pays you per the hour. Today helping the neighbour lady in her garden is now replaced by being employed at a nursery taking care of saplings , and receiving a salary on the basis of a monthly payment.

The fundamentals of work remain the same. The first requirement is investing your time and effort into your job, whether physical or mental. In some cases, the sole effort needed to invest in the job is economic in the sense of e.g. making money in a business but it requires physical and mental commitment at a certain level.

Over the years changing of the primary essential has been more psychological than physical. Mine work, farm work and fishing have slowly been replaced by desk jobs. The power of our minds that's been getting more attention than that of the brute muscle. Thanks to the advancement of technology and the rise of technology, more emphasis is being given to the human mind and it is the most powerful tool when it comes to determine the future and shape the future of our society.

Around a century back, the society's primary importance was the production of goods to meet the basic requirements. It was the time that the printing presses and assembly lines had just been created. The primary reason for the job was to assist the community endure. The luxury items weren't essential, they were things to entertain yourself in leisurewhich isn't something we are surrounded in a lot today.

The goal of those who worked jobs was to be able to endure the competition. As technology progressed and science, mankind began exploring new methods of reducing the physical exertion required. This required the use of the human brain in the beginning and was followed by a routine manual procedure that demanded pushing buttons and giving a couple of instructions.

Relaxing and letting the new worker just sit back and enjoy the latest method of churning out outstanding results. It was at this point that man saw the present-day blessing to all workplacesand workplaces - technology. He believed that the day would come that all a job could need was to whisper the manual instructions or following an established standard procedure and do the 'job'.

The other essential aspect of a job's pay. The development of money into a universal method of payment for all things has played a significant role during this period. People used to trim their gardens to feel the satisfaction of the task, or even to improve their surroundings. Today, jobs that are not difficult to perform like babysitting can be paid and requires the hiring of random teens who promise to watch over the children while you're off in exchange for dollars.

The pleasure of working has been replaced by the desire for the need for currency. It is not surprising that money is the primary source of income for our times and any changes that are to be made must be first addressed with regard to the effects of money and its cousins in terms of causes and. The other essential aspect is that of economic remuneration is the major reason for jobs, and the reason why people choose these over other jobs that only brings you satisfaction.

The third and final essential of an occupation is the existence of an employer as well as an employee. Two roles must be fulfilled. The first is that of the master or boss, the one who directs another person to complete the task. The master is also responsible for giving the second important money to the other. The other party plays the second part of the deal. He gets an instruction from the employer and executes the task required to gain the financial benefit that is promised. If the task is completed successfully, the job will result in economic success. Both roles have to be in sync with one and the job isn't an employment in the true sense. A possible exception to the crucial is the self-employed who don't work for or for any employer , but they can argue that they fulfill both two roles of employer and employee.

A job today is no longer a definition in the book that was prevalent in the past. It's no longer simply a contract between an employer and employee with the aim of getting the job done. It has expanded and expanded its scope to include other significant aspects such as employee-employer relations and the right of employees to take holidays and holidays, the obligation of employers to pay the employee remuneration, and other stipulations that are deeply embedded.

The traditional system of a simple structure has now been replaced with a more constructive realm, in where not only the function of the person doing the job is defined, however, the person's inter - and intra-personal activities along with a number of other elements are also listed.

Chapter 13: Being Confident

It's not unusual to be nervous prior to an interview.

Employers are looking for confidence and self-assurance.

How can you assist yourself to feel as confident as you possibly can?

A) PREPARATION

If you're prepared you will be more confident.

Knowing what you can offer will make you feel confident about yourself.

A reminder note in your file for the interview can make you feel more confident.

Understanding what you are trying to communicate will help you are more at ease.

Knowing about the organization prior to the event will allow you to be confident about it.

Being aware of the questions you wish to ask eliminates another source of confusion.

Looking good makes you feel good.

B) RELAXATION

Relaxation techniques can aid in interview preparation as well as other occasions.

Make sure you have enough time before the interview Do not be stressed.

Relaxation techniques are best practiced with regular exercise.

The feeling of nervousness (hands sweating, a twisted stomach, frigid feet) can be described as a bodily reaction to what our mind perceives as danger (fight and fight)

Find a relaxing technique that you like and use it regularly.

Below are a few suggestions of techniques for relaxation can be beneficial to you.

Relaxation Techniques

If stress takes over your nervous system , your body is inundated with chemicals that help prepare you for "fight or fight". Although the stress response may save your life in situations when you have to react swiftly, it wears your body out when it is continuously activated by the stress of daily life. Its relaxation reaction puts brakes on this increased level of alertness and helps bring your mind and body back to a level of balance.

There isn't a single relaxation technique that is suitable for all. When choosing a technique for relaxation take into consideration your individual requirements and preferences, your fitness level and how you react to stress. The best relaxation method is one that you find appealing and fits with your lifestyle and can help you focus your thoughts and interrupt your thoughts every day in order to trigger a relaxation response.

Many different methods of relaxation can help restore your nervous system to equilibrium by triggering your relaxation reaction. The relaxation response isn't sitting down on the sofa or laying down but rather a mental activity that makes the body feel at peace, calm and concentrated.

The basics of these techniques for relaxation isn't easy, but it does require a lot of time and practice. The majority of stress experts suggest making time for minimum 10-20 minutes each day for your relaxing routine. If you'd like additional relief from stress try to set a goal of 30 to one hour. If you think that's an overwhelming task, keep in mind that many of these strategies can be integrated into your routine and practiced at your desk during lunch or while riding the bus on your commute to work.

Relaxation Technique 1

Meditation on breathing to relieve stress

With its emphasis on deep clean breaths deep breathing is a simple yet effective, relaxation method. It's simple to master and practice virtually anywhere, and is a the fastest way to bring your stress levels under control. Deep breathing is the foundation of many other practices for relaxation also, and it can be combined with other relaxation aspects like aromatherapy and music. All you need is a few minutes , and an area to stretch.

Practicing deep breathing meditation

The most important thing to do for deep breathing is to breath deeply from your abdomen, allowing the most fresh air feasible in your lungs. If you breathe deeply from your abdomen instead of taking shallow breaths from your chest's upper part to inhale oxygen, you'll get more oxygen. The higher the amount of oxygen you take in more relaxed, less feeling short of breath and nervous you feel.

Relax and sit back straight. Place the palm of your hand onto your chest, and the other one on your stomach.

Breathe via your nostrils. The stomach of your hand should be raised. The hand that is on your chest should only move a little.

Inhale through your mouth by pushing out as the air you can while contraction of those abdominal muscles. Your stomach's hand will move as you exhale. However, your hand on your other side should move tiny.

Continue breathing in through your nose, and exhale to exhale through the mouth. Make sure to breathe in enough that your abdomen's lower part increases and decreases. Slowly count as you exhale.

If you have difficulty breathing out of your abdomen while sitting up, consider lying down on the floor. Lay a small piece of paper on your stomach and then try breathing so your book is raised when you inhale , and falls down as you exhale.

Relaxation technique 2

Progressive muscle relaxation to relieve stress

Progressive muscle relaxation is an ensuing two-step process where you gradually relax and tense various muscle groups throughout the body.

Through regular practice, gradual muscle relaxation can give you a deep understanding of the way tension -- and complete relaxation feels like in various parts of your body. This knowledge helps you recognize and eliminate the initial signs of tension in the muscles caused by stress. As your body relaxes and your mind relaxes, so does your body. It is possible to combine deep breathing and progressive muscle relaxation to achieve an another level of relaxation.

Practicing progressive muscle relaxation

Before you begin practicing Progressive Muscle Relaxation, speak with your doctor if are prone to back issues, muscle spasms or any other serious injuries that can be aggravated through tensing muscles.

The majority of progressive muscle relaxation practitioners begin at the feet , and progress to the face.

Untie your clothes remove your shoes and then get comfy.

Relax for a few minutes and calm yourself, breathing through and out slowly deep breaths.

If you're calm and ready to get started with your focus on the right side of your foot. Spend a few moments focusing on the way your foot feels.

Slowly contract the muscles in your right foot and squeeze as hard as you are able to. Do this for a total of 10.

Let your foot relax on your left. Concentrate on the tension that is dissolving and the way your foot feels when it loosens and becomes limp.

Relax in this state for a few seconds breathe deeply and take it slow.

Once you're ready switch your attention towards your left leg. Repeat the same sequence of relaxation and tension.

Slowly move your body, releasing and contracting the muscles as you move.

It could take some time at first, but do not to tighten muscles that are not the same than the ones you intend to.

Chapter 14: Sample Thank-You Letters

Appreciation is an integral part of every day communication. It's when we acknowledge and express gratitude to someone else for what they've done for us, or for something that they've given us. "Thank you" or "thank-you" are among the first words we are taught. They're often referred to as "the magical words" together with "please" as well as "excuse for me."

It is possible to ask why you should be thanking someone for doing something they're paid to do regardless, like thanking the waiter for serving meals or the service attendant who pumps your gasoline. Recognizing and appreciating the work performed for us shows that we're aware of the effort and time put into by the other person in attending to us. It is a sign that we don't consider it a given that they have chosen to spend the precious resource of their time with us and not doing something else. It's our way of demonstrating gratitude for the risk they paid to spend time with us instead of making a different or even more lucrative utilization of their time and other resources. Similar to when someone offers us anything for any reason. Giving them a thank-you is not expensive and helps the person who provided the service feel appreciated and acknowledged.

A Detailed Interview Process

The process of interviewing is lengthy and complex. It begins when an organization is aware of the necessity of filling a specific job. They create a custom job advertisement that aims to draw the most qualified candidates while dispelling candidates that aren't. Then, they narrow down the ones whose education as well as their professional experience are most compatible with their needs. Then, they invite them for an interview.

Most of the time the interview will be divided into several sections. It could be an oral or written interview. oral interview and, when the job is technical, candidates might be required to go through an interview in a practical setting to demonstrate their expertise and skills on the job. Candidates who are successful are then taken by the organization as employees new to the company.

From a candidate's point of point of view, the interview process starts when they realize they are ready to enter the workforce fully. The next step is to determine what kind of job to seek according to their skills and qualifications. In the current extremely competitive marketplace, the job search could be overwhelming and even depressing. Once a potential candidate has made a decision on what they'd like to do regarding job name and responsibilities and responsibilities, they can then browse the numerous online job websites and boards or contact an employment agency to search for a job.

There are additional factors to be considered in addition to what is the geographical location for the business or the unit with the job, as well as the type of benefits are offered, if any, the business offers its employees. Certain candidates might choose big multinational corporations as opposed to family-owned businesses for many reasons. Following that, you need waiting for an interview phone call. It could come directly from the hiring firm's Human Resource Department, or an outside party when they've engaged an agency to recruit. The applicant should have conducted prior research regarding the employer.

However, before the interview arrives, it's sensible to review the information regarding the company, paying particular attention to the processes of the department to which the candidate worked. Candidates must ensure that they're equipped in terms of appropriate clothes and get enough sleep prior to the night. In some firms both oral and written interviews take place in the exact same time.

The behavioral interview is conducted in conjunction with the interview. The applicant is asked questions to evaluate their behavior by reference to their past experiences as well as hypothetical situations. Based on the candidates' responses, the company chooses the one that is the most suitable for their personality and temperament. most closely to their corporate vision and needs.

After the interview it isn't quite over for the applicant. It is generally recommended to write a thank you note to the interviewerthanking them for the time they took with you. In some situations such as when there are two applicants who share other areas, a timely written thank-you note could be able to break the tie and ensure the spot for the applicant.

A thank you note must be concise and sincere. thank the person who interviewed you for your time. repeat what you have said during the interview that you think makes you stand out from the other candidates, and indicate that you are eager to learn what to expect from the following steps in the process. The letter could be written in hand or printed. It could also be an email.

General Thank-You Letter Outline

This is a general outline of a thank-you letter following a successful behavioral test.

"Re: "Thank you for your consideration"

Begin with a personal greeting (such as"Dear Mr. Smith," or "Hello Kenneth,") this is appropriate since you've already spoken to the person you are contacting and developed a relationship with them.

After your introduction, you can open the body of your letter to express your appreciation for their time while the interview was conducted.

Include a specific item that you talked about during the interview that caught your attention. This shows your employer that this letter was customized specifically for them.

Inform them of your interest in the position and let them know that you are eager to hear details about next steps of the process.

Make them aware that they shouldn't hesitate to call you if they have you have any concerns or queries in the interim.

It is also possible to include an explanation of your reasons for why you think you are able to succeed in this job.

Following are examples on how you can write different thank you letters dependent on the business or industry, following having passed a behavioral interview.

Letter Sample 1: Business Thank-You Letter in formal format. Letter

A formal thank you letter should be ideally one page. It is recommended to write it for an established company that has an unwavering and established procedure. They tend to be a fan of formality and adhere to established processes and procedures for their work.

Your names

Address Line 1

Line 2 Address

Date

Name of the Interviewer

The Job Title of the Interviewer

Name of the company

Line 1 of the Company's Address

Line 2 of the Address of the Company.

Hello Mr./Ms. Surname

RE: Thank you for your time

Thank you so much for the opportunity to conduct an interview in your organization for the post of [title of position yesterday. I really enjoyed the discussion and am grateful for the chance to gain more insight into the company. I am extremely interested in the position and am looking forward to joining your team.

After discussing it the possibility, it seems as a great combination of my abilities and experience, as well as the demands of the business. You stated that you require an individual with skills in [insert here] and I have a wealth of knowledge of [insert here ability or experience essential to the position.It is also important to have Additionally I have expertise of [insert here experience that is uniquespecific experience. I have developed [insert specific ability or combination of abilitiesin my current or previous] position in [previous or current job] that is required for your job title job title.

Thank you again for taking the time to consider me for this amazing job opportunity. I am prepared and eager to answer any questions you may have. Please do not hesitate to contact me with any questions , concerns or if you require more details. I look forward getting in touch with you and would love to be part of your team soon.

Best Regards,

[Your name]

[Your address]

Sample Letter 2. Small to Medium Enterprise Thank You Letter

Small to Medium Enterprises (SMEs) tend to be more flexible when it comes to their structures and systems, so they can use a semi-formal thank-you card that could suffice, like the one provided below.

Your names

Address Line 1

Line 2 Address

Date

Name of the interviewer

The job title of an interviewer

The name of the company

Line 1 for Address of the Company.

Line 2 of the Address of the Company.

Dear Interviewer's First Name

RE: Thank you for your time

I am grateful to you taking time from working schedules to talk to me on the phone yesterday regarding the job title [insert Job Title] at [insert Name of Companycompany name]. It was an extremely informative conversation, and it was enjoyable to listen to all the details you thoroughly discussed regarding the requirements for this job.

The details you provided about [a particular aspect of the job you applied for] was particularly intriguing.

I am sure that my unique expertise will allow me in settling in and excel in this position which is a job I am eagerly looking forward to entering.

I'm looking forward to hearing from you on the next steps of the process. Please be free to reach me at any time should you have any queries.

Thank you once again. I am hoping for a response from you sooner rather than later. long.

Best Regards,

[Your Name]

Sample Letter 3: Start-Ups

Tech companies and startups are very relaxed in regards to formality. They don't mind quick, succinct, casual communications. They also are very tech-oriented, so sending them long letters could make you unqualified from an interview with them.

Your names

Address Line 1

Line 2 of Address

Date

Name of the interviewer

Job Title for Interviewers

The Name of the Company

Address of the company line 1.

Line 2 for Address of the company.

Hello [Interviewer's Name]

RE: Thank you for your time

I would like to take this time to express my gratitude for the time you took [on Tuesday]I would like to thank you for your time [on Monday]. I gained many things from our discussion on [a specific subject you spoke aboutand also appreciated the insights into the job title you discussed.

It's certainly an thrilling opportunity which look to excel and succeed in! I'm eager to hear more updates about the same. In the meantime, please do not hesitate to reach me with any queries or want to clarify anything.

Thank you for the wonderful discussion.

Best Regards,

[Your Name]

Things to Note:

Be sure to write a thank-you note as soon as you can after your interview. It is recommended to send it within 24 hours of the interview so that you're still remembered by the interviewer.

* Each of these templates can be customized and then sent via email. This is by removing all address lines, and using "RE:" as the subject line.

Make sure you double-check the spelling of your handwritten letters . You can also do spell-checking with your word processor to check for printed letters to ensure your letter is free of errors which could result in embarrassment, or even result in you losing your job in the end!

Handwritten letters feel more authentic, however you should be cautious not to create a long letter by hand. It can appear messy, which can impact the comprehension and readability of the note.

Thank-you letters to each interviewer must be unique and tailored to the specifics of that specific date and the particular interview. The above guidelines are guidelines only which shouldn't duplicated and then re-used into any situation.

Use sincerity to convey your feelings using genuine, yet professional language.

Be sure to show interest as well as enthusiasm within your email. Cite relevant portions of the discussion , and show you are keen to join the business, but at the same time be sure not to appear overly desperate or needy.

Include something that's not on your cover letter or resume.

Make sure you've completed your due diligence by researching everything possible about the business in advance, during and after your interview to ensure that you write the best thank-you note for the company.

After you've written your thank-you note, now you must wait for the business to respond according to the time they had stated. If they don't yet, it's okay to call them and follow up at the time you agreed to However, remember that many other activities could be happening behind the scenes and the delay they experience does not always mean that it is bad for you. It might take some time to make a final conclusion, which is why your check-ins must be scheduled, but at least not once every hour, or day.

Be on top of your job search, even if you are waiting for a response from a company that you submitted an application to or have an interview. You may land your ideal job before other applicants have decided.

Chapter 15: Practice is the key to perfecting your skills

While in high school I was in the public speaking course where students had to present in front of the class and deliver five minutes of persuasive presentations about a controversial subject. I believed I was well-prepared and had enough evidence to convince my classmates who were skeptical of my views to agree with mine. I had images of a tragic story, as well as shocking figures, but I was unable to practice my presentation before presenting. I thought that the topic was so shocking that I could manage to fill the space with the data I found, and be able to improvise the rest of the presentation. I came up with the presentation lasted about three minutes with eyes that were blank on my classmates on their faces, and a less convincing argument than I believed I could have. It was not my best performance.

Like any other performance or contest it is essential to ensure that your technique is perfected prior to being in the spotlight, with everyone's attention on you. You need to give flawlessly, demonstrating that you're prepared and confident. The interviewer has to sit through a handful of interviews every day, and asking the same question multiple times and getting the same responses. Take that breath of fresh air that catches the attention of interviewers from the very beginning by presenting a assured smile, strong handshake, and the appropriate attire. Make them remember you by your persuasive answers and charismatic personality.

A Story from Someone Else

Don't be the broken record that your HR manager heard numerous times before. Think about what the most well-known answer would be, then make improvements to it, or modify your answer completely. Sometimes, the most common answers are popular because they're popular and acceptable. But, if the answers become too preferred by prospective employers, it could appear that candidates took the easy route to get. The interviewer will not only already have seen the same responses previously, but they'll be bored by your routine answers, and may be dissatisfied by your inability to think outside the box. If the position you're applying for offers the potential to advance or managerial responsibilities the employer is likely to seek a candidate with leadership skills who can think and speak their mind.

Make sure you give thoughtful answers which reflect your preparedness in the face of an interview. There's a difference between sounding like you've been prepared. Practice with a family member, or at the bathroom mirror. Make sure you practice until you feel comfortable with your answers.

Mirror, Mirror

I'm a fervent mirror-talker. I like to be in front of my reflection and observe how I appear when I have different reactions or expressions. When I put on my makeup in the morning my husband will see me playing with my facial expressions and talking with myself about nothing (and often in various accents). Get comfortable with yourself, and be aware of the way you look, and what you sound like. Develop your voice's tones and volumes. Make sure to be funny in your reflection, even when others are watching. If you're more at ease with yourself and get in your own naivety your more relaxed you'll feel in different environments and situations.

If you're struggling with speaking about yourself to the mirror, to observe your facial expressions and reactions start with something simpler. Choose your most loved song and sing along. Make it appear as if you're at a stage before a large audience and let them know that you're passionate about the songs lyrics. It's fine to be silly--in fact, it's encouraged! Be at ease in your own skin Building confidence and confidence, which will be a source of energy during your interview.

It's an overwhelming amount of things to consider in preparation for an interview, but these exercises can help you in the confines of the workplace. They can help you become more confident and assertive in personal and professional interactions.

Expression

When I was a young child my dad would play an activity with me and my sisters known as "faces. He would shout out a face and we had to create the same smile. "Happy Face!" and we'd put the most dazzling smiling faces on the face, showing every single one of our teeth. "Angry Face!" and we'd raise our eyebrows, squint our eyes and close our mouths pulling our chins back to our chests.

Although it was originally a children's game that helped us improve our communication skills and to communicate our feelings It is a wonderful game in preparing for interviews. Since the actual reactions and expressions you'll have will be less obvious similar to what you're doing. Check out what you do when confronted with information, regardless of whether it's stimulating or not. You may be surprised by the way your responses don't show up in conversation in the way you believe they will (or contrary to that, they may seem too strongly). I've interviewed many people who looked as if they were staring at me all the time. They seemed completely empty; even though I'm sure they were engaged in the conversation. Keep in mind that a blank expression or a lack of facial expressions could be perceived as boring or uninterested. Who wants to employ an employee who isn't excited about the job or the company?

Voice Inflection Volume, Pronunciation and Voice

It's so crucial that you are heard. You should not just make yourself heard however, you should also try to express your thoughts clearly to ensure you're completely heard. We've all tried to communicate with someone who is unable to understand what they are saying. You either have to ask "what? " after each phrase or you simply stop and look at your phone, pretending to know what's being said and trying to get to leave the conversation. While being aware of how you speak You should also be aware of how you alter your voice's inflection.

I've been through many interviews with candidates that spoke with such a dreadful monotone that I was bored to listen to their responses. Particularly, the job I was seeking to hire for required an excellent quality in customer care. It was not possible that I would let someone who spoke monotone in the interview to converse with my customers. I'd lose business!

While you pay attention to your voice's inflection, you can experiment with the different ranges in your voice. Of course, you wouldn't wish to flit around excessively when interviewing and sounding like a cartoon animated cartoon, but you should not remain in one constant tone all the time. If you can play with the different levels of your voice's inflection it will allow you to emphasize the most important points you wish to emphasize during the interview and let the interviewer know that you are actively involved with the interview.

Inflection and volume are two things that go hand-in-hand. In normal conversations, you'll notice that most of the time we tend to drop the words at the end of sentences. We were taught in elementary school that when we get at the end of a sentence, we must lower our voice to signify the beginning of the period. The issue with this rule during interviews is that, often we'll stumble over the endings of sentences leaving the sentence's conclusion unclear. We were also instructed to raise our vocal pitch when we ask questions to indicate an inquiry mark.

It's time to shake things up you've learned, try raising your voice when you get near the end of your sentence, and let it out.

It's not meant to turn it into a query or anything, but instead to eliminate the mumbled ending in this manner:

I was employed there for 4 years.

It is still possible to present an ending to your answer however, this way your final answer won't be erased. This is an excellent exercise to try out with a person you know or recording your own. Look up any book, magazine or pamphlet, and then read one page while trying to raise your voice to give a powerful conclusion for your paragraphs. You'll see a marked distinction.

Nervous Ticks

Everybody has their own ticks of nerves. The term "nervous tick" refers to any action you do in your subconscious to help keep your nerves in check or to remain focussed. The only drawback lies in the fact that ticks can be repeated physical actions that show that nerves are active. Sometimes we get ticks in order in order to avoid answering questions or come up with the right words to use however it distracts from the actual questions.

My nervous tick was putting into "uhh" throughout my conversations. At first I didn't know how many times I'd disrupt my thought process. When I recorded myself on my own, I was awestruck by how uncomfortable this sound made my responses. Instead of being able to hear the words I spoke on the tape I became distracted by the number of occasions the "uhh" entered my voice. My issue is that the brain functioned faster than I could talk, and I'd end up falling over my words or creating a space for me to slow down and speak. To fix this issue I tried slowing down my responses and consciously selecting the words, and avoiding space that could be filled with.

Other typical ticks include clearing your throat prior to every answer and frequently doing hair-dos or making certain hand gestures repeatedly and spaces to fill in ("umm"/"uhh") as well as leg bobbing or the habit of touching or touching yourself, touching your your legs and many others. Be aware of ticks within yourself which could distract you away from the conversation.

The Moment You Step Through the Door

As soon as you walk through the door to your office, the interview is about to begin (and an important note that that time should be prior to the time scheduled of the meeting). "Being on time" means that you have checked on with the desk clerk around 5-10 minutes before the scheduled interview time. This demonstrates the qualities of managing time and accountability. Don't allow your interviewer to wait for you to finish. If you want to be punctual there are some points to think about when you are getting ready for your interview: Set your alarm clock to get you up early to allow you time to dress and double-check all of your materials for the interview. Check directions to the office of the interviewer the night prior to. Examine the traffic report and allow for sufficient time to drive.

Let's admit it. Life occurs. If something happens that leaves you in a position that you are certain you will not get to the interview on time, make sure you call ahead and promptly explain your circumstances and where you are. It's better that the interviewer is aware that you are likely to be late than anticipated than to believe you're not really good at managing your time.

Make sure you are friendly with everyone who is at the reception counter, be friendly, and smile at people who happen to pass by as you wait for your interview. You don't know who your direct supervisor will be after you've been hired It is best to begin your work relationship with a professional manner. My boss was sure that I was at his desk and shut the door as candidates came in for an interview. He would ask me to stand at the front desk and observe about the candidate as they waited in line for him. They didn't realize they were being questioned and examined by me. I am much younger than I am and was less intimidating to have an exchange. There was no doubt that I had a say in the selection process.

One woman who was due to an interview was informed that she was scheduled to meet with my boss, who was a man. The woman arrived in tight, unrevealing clothing with hair curled and teased with a thick red lipstick. She approached me and demanded that I "let me know I'm here, dear." I was stunned by that. She proceeded to blow-dry her hair and reposition her...assets...while in the waiting room for my boss to arrive. It sounded like something out of a movie that's not good However I've seen it all. It's no surprise that she didn't be hired.

If you are hired for that job you'll be in close contact with everyone in the office. You'll spend a lot of time with them and they're all deserving of the highest respect. Each of them has a distinct personality. There are various personality types that are perfectly suited to certain jobs. Your success will bedetermined, in part, the way you are able to succeed when working with ALL kinds of personalities. If you can, at least, be sure to show your (future) colleagues respect because you all work toward the same goal.

Let Me Listen to Your Body Talk to Me

If the words coming out of your mouth are insightful and absorbent What do your body language is communicating? If you are using your body language in the wrong way, your body language could transmit contradicting messages to the interviewer.

I was interviewing a candidate that was excellent on paper and was with a polished appearance. He engaged me well by his answers and impressed me by his understanding of the company's culture, however there was one factor that slowed his chances of being selected by his body language. The candidate was slouched in his seat, put one feet on the table, avoided eye contact, and even paused my questions to give me answers. His body language suggested the candidate didn't want to talk to me, and his shrewd manner of speaking came across as arrogant and rude.

He was too familiar with the interview process routine. He took every step in preparing himself to answer questions in the meeting, however, he failed to keep his professional appearance. He appeared as if I was wasting my time by asking the same questions others who were interested in hiring had been asked in previous interviews. Even if this was only the fifteenth time he was interviewed the same person, he ought to have treated it as if it was his first and sole.

Be conscious about your posture and your stature. Stand straight and make eye contact with the interviewer and display your best professional side while engaging them in conversations. You should nod your head in agreement as you listen to the interviewer describe the role and the requirements for the skill and ask questions if you don't know what they're discussing. Allow your body to speak as loudly as you speak.

If this particular candidate been paying the attention of the way I move, he might be aware of my displeasure with his attitude and my waning enthusiasm for his work.

Chapter 16: Common Interview Mistakes

If you are able to educate yourself and avoid these errors, you'll significantly increase your chances of an interview that is successful and ultimately getting the job you've always wanted. These aren't difficult to do, but it requires the commitment and knowledge. Once you are aware of the things you could be doing wrong, you'll be able recognize the areas you've been a failure before.

Unprofessional attire is among the first things an interviewer will observe. It may seem acceptable to wear a t-shirt and jeans to an interview , since you don't have anything more formal. However, jeans are not appropriate to wear for an interview, unless the interview is held at the site of construction or an unclean warehouse, and just if your interviewer has told you prior to your interview that the area will be filthy. There's no acceptable moment to wear shorts for an interview, or even a shorts-style outfit, and this includes Capri's of any length. The most appropriate attire during an interview (unless otherwise specified) are blouses and skirts as well as dresses and dress shorts and shirts for ladies, and casual slacks or dressy pants with dress-y shirts for men.

Ringing your phone in an interview is another thing which could ruin your successful interview. If you are unable to put your phone away in the vehicle, at least show the grace to turn off the phone or switch it into silent mode. If it's not a life-threatening situation involving your child or relatives it is not something that should be left to be kept until the time of the interview has ended. While you are in the interview, you shouldn't be carrying your mobile phone at your side or on your table. It is not advisable to make use of your mobile phone during the interview, any more than you would bring your children to an interview. This is another thing that can make a company cross you off as a potential candidate in a short time. If you can't locate a babysitter for an interview, then you don't have the desire to go to work all day.

Company Research

If you are scheduled for interviews with a business you're not acquainted with, conduct some research. In the majority of interviews, the interviewer will ask what you think you could do to help their business. It can be extremely difficult to answer this question if you don't have any knowledge about the topic. You can find a amount of details by going to their website and learning about their history and mission statement. It's also a great time to check whether their mission and vision is similar to yours and is something you'd like to be part of.

If you don't have access to computers at home or at work, visit the library to find out more information about the business you're thinking of working. While it might seem insignificant at the moment, you'll benefit by learning more about the business. It proves you've done your research and that you're truly interested in their business. If there's a choice needed to make between yourself and an individual who has not been able to find out details about the business and its products, you will earn more points on the final assessment.

If you discover something about the business, you will discern whether you'll be an appropriate fit for the company and if you truly want to work for the company. In the interview process, it is possible that you will not always have an accurate picture of the business and you don't need to ask questions or confess that you didn't do any research. The more information you have about the business, the easier it will be for both you as well as the person interviewing you to determine whether you're a suitable match for the job that you're applying to. Sometimes , it's not feasible to conduct a significant amount of research, but you have to gather enough information in order to convince the interviewer that you've at a minimum known about the company and understand the products they offer or offerings.

It is also essential to learn about the company you're considering working as they could be associated with causes which you are not convinced in. For instance that they are in favor of animal testing and you're opposed to any type tests on animals then you may be hesitant regarding being employed by the company. If you are aware of these types of issues prior to the interview, or, at a minimum, prior to the hiring process is over, you should be sure to avoid an organization whose values do not match your own.

How to Control the Interview Conversation

One of the issues that many individuals face is controlling the interview conversation so that it is in line with professional subjects. Engaging with the interviewer in a intimate conversations is not likely to earn you extra points. In fact, it could even cause you to lose credibility since it appears as if you're trying to gain the job by forming relationships and the recruiter. Of of course, the interviewer is not completely faultless as often interviewers will ask personal questions. If you engage in conversations that cover personal matters, it impedes the objective in the conversation. This will hinder you from getting the full reason for the interview.

Conclusion

There are a lot of questions that an interviewer could ask, but you'd be surprised to discover that the majority of them are based on (or are connected to) those we've discussed in this article.

Simply put, once you have an excellent understanding of the different topics we've covered and you're not going to have anything to fret about. You will be able to go into any interview with the most confidence possible, confident that you'll be astonished by all the interviewers and land the job.

Be sure to do everything that we have talked about and include a thorough study of all the areas we have identified.